Visualization of Interface Metaphor for Software:
An Engineering Approach

Dinesh S. Katre

DISSERTATION.COM

Boca Raton

Visualization of Interface Metaphor for Software:
An Engineering Approach

Dissertation.com
Boca Raton, Florida
USA • 2011

ISBN-10: 1-59942-377-4
ISBN-13: 978-1-59942-377-7

प्रज्ञा विवेकं लभते भित्रैरागमदर्शने ः।
कियद्धा शक्यमुन्नेतुं स्वतर्कमनुधावता ।।

भर्तृहरि : वाक्यपदीय

By adopting and sharing multi-disciplinary approach,
knowledge is transformed into wisdom.
How much can one imagine by simply employing one's own logic?

Bhartruhari, Vākyapadiya, 5th Century AD

Acknowledgements

I am very grateful to my supervisor Dr. Mukul K. Sinha, Managing Director, Expert Software Consultant Ltd., New Delhi for mentoring me with compassion during the five years of doctoral research. He is the key motivator for me, who recognized my interest in research and boosted my spirit to work harder in that direction. I am thankful to him for his valuable guidance, counseling and help in difficult situations.

I am extremely thankful to C-DAC for its consistent support and encouragement to me during this research.

It is beyond my capacity to even express how much I owe to *Saint Dnyaneshwar (1275-1296),* whose metaphorical verses from *Dnyaneshwari* kept me enchanted for so many years and have been a great source of inspiration for me in this research on interface metaphors. I thank Sri Sakhare Maharaj for helping me in understanding the spiritual metaphors from *Dnyaneshwari.* I am indebted to Dr. Vijay Bhatkar, founder Executive Director of C-DAC, who entrusted the responsibility of multimedia rendering of *Dnyaneshwari* and introduced me to Shri Sakhare Maharaj.

I am grateful to Dr. Aaron Marcus, President, Aaron Marcus Associates, USA for appreciating my efforts and guiding me during his visit to India. I reproduce his comments on one of my articles [Katre, 2002] related to this dissertation as "I have for a long time thought that India and China might produce new applications that derived their metaphors from local culture/history/literature. Your article points the way. What seemed intriguing was to view a list of these metaphors and religious/historical references, and to compare them with some standard Western approaches. Your comparison at the end of categories or types of metaphors was useful." I am so thankful to him for his encouraging remarks and highlighting the uniqueness of this work.

I am thankful to Prof. V. N. Jha, Director, Center for Advanced Study in Sanskrit, University of Pune for sharing the knowledge of linguistic metaphors in *Vedic* literature. I also thank Dr. Mrs. Jha for providing appropriate reference from *Vedic* literature related to metaphors. I am extremely thankful to Prof. K. Srinivas Rao from IMSc, Chennai for his wisdom tips and guidance in improving my writing skills.

I am thankful to Film and Television Institute, Pune, SNDT University, Mumbai and Industrial Design Center, Indian Institute of Technology, Mumbai for organizing my lectures on the topic of research.

I express gratitude to Birla Institute of Technology and Science (BITS), Pilani for offering an opportunity to a professional like me to pursue research through its off-campus doctoral program. I also thank the staff of BITS, Pilani namely Dr. Ravi Prakash, Dean, Research and Consultancy division; Dr. Rahul Banerjee, Dr. Shan Balasubramanian and Dr. S. D. Pohekar for their guidance and support.

I am indebted to my colleague and friend Mr. Devashish Pandya for volunteering to be a sounding board for my ideas. He always brought new insights to me while brainstorming and debating with him. I also thank all the subjects who patiently participated in the tests that I performed and provided their valuable inputs.

Last but not the least, I gratefully acknowledge the trademarks belonging to their owners that are mentioned during our discussion and also the creators of the UI screenshots which are used as examples in appendices.

Dinesh S. Katre

Table of Contents

APPENDICES

List of Tables & Figures

Abbreviations

HCI   Human-Computer Interaction
UXD   User Experience Design
CIM   Candidate Interface Metaphor
CDM   Cross-Domain Mappings
UCs   Unmapped Concepts
URs   Unmapped Requirements
CTP   Commentary of Task Performance
IPS   Interface Play Script
DT   Dissection Termination
UDL   User Domain Lexicon
ADL   Application Domain Lexicon
UI   User Interface
IPS   Interface Play Script
SDLC Software Development Life Cycle
UCD   User Centered Design
UEM   Usability Evaluation Method

Abstract

This dissertation presents a comprehensive process for **visualization of interface metaphor** for software, which is helpful in designing interactive user interfaces with magical super-affordances and definitive user experiences. The steps of this process are integrated with the **Waterfall Model of Software Development Life Cycle (SDLC).** It mainly focuses on **pre-facto analysis, quantitative and qualitative evaluation** of interface metaphor to be performed during **Requirements Engineering (RE).** In this, the *candidate interface metaphors* are identified within the **common knowledge dimensions** of specified users. **Commentary of Task Performance (CTP)** and **Interface Play Script (IPS)** are written similar to a drama script; and then juxtaposed for capturing the **mental model** and **sensory details** of the tasks. The *candidate interface metaphors* are classified as **coherent** and **diverse** based on the interrelationships coded in the **cognitive map**. The conceptual structures are further categorized at different levels as **Domain, Conglomerate, Multitudinous, Singleton (Inanimate, Animate),** and **Flat Concepts** to help in assessing their potential. Various aspects of the selected *candidate interface metaphors* are identified and tuned based on the determinants of software and user for crafting the desired user experiences. The **analysis** of interface metaphor is performed through its **concept-by-concept dissection**. **Cross-Domain Mappings (CDMs)** are formed between the **resonating** metaphoric concepts and software requirements. The dissected conceptual structure is quantified to identify the **Cross-Domain Mappings (CDMs), Unmapped Concepts (UCs), Unmapped Requirements (URs), Usable Conceptual Bandwidth and Coverage.** After this **User** and **Application Domain Lexicons** are built to help in designing the **linguistic metaphors** to be used in the user interface. Interdisciplinary **Usability Heuristics** and **Usability Indicators** are identified for the **qualitative evaluation** of interface metaphor. **Quantitative metrics** is provided for quantifying the results of heuristic evaluation. Interface metaphor is given a **tangible form** through multimedia rendering. The documents and artifacts generated through the visualization process are linked with it for corroboration of results. Usability heuristics are applied and tested on the multimedia rendering. A **Remote Usability Testing method** is developed for evaluating the cross-cultural issues. The interface metaphor is then accepted for incorporation in the design of software after satisfactory clearance through usability evaluations and tests.

Chapter 1. Introduction

This dissertation presents a comprehensive process for **visualization of interface metaphor** for software applications. The steps of this process are integrated with the **Waterfall Model of Software Development Life Cycle (SDLC)**. This process is designed to help the **interface designers** and **user experience designers** in performing **pre-facto analysis** and **usability evaluation** of **Candidate Interface Metaphors (CIMs)** *in the formative stages of software development.* It also helps the **software developers** in specifying the **software requirements** with full awareness of the proposed interface metaphor during the **Requirements Engineering (RE)** stage itself.

The **user interface** provides an effective **communication medium** between a human and a computer [Pressman, 2001]. User interfaces are designed with metaphors as they help you understand one thing in terms of the other [Lakoff et al., 1980]. A metaphor highlights similarities between the known and the unknown (user interface). In the context of this dissertation, the term **visualization** is to be interpreted as formation of mental visual images. This definition has acquired more meaning in terms of the recall and imagination of all **sensory experiences** [Owen, 1999].

Chapter 2 presents the arguments in different categories for defining the problem statement of this dissertation. **The present understanding of the software community about application of interface metaphor is mostly based on post-facto analysis of successful software products.** The researchers have stated that there isn't **adequate guidance** available for finding suitable interface metaphors [Vaantinen, 1994] [Smilowitz, 1996] and for carrying out its **pre-facto analysis** [Madsen, 1994]. There are several other related issues that remain to be addressed such as the **theoretical basis for selection** of interface metaphor [Madsen, 1994] [Smilowitz, 1996], the method for its **optimization, evaluation** and its **qualitative study** [Marcus, 1994, 1998] [Vaantinen, 1994]. Also, there is a need to measure the ***applicability*** and ***potential*** of a metaphor [Palmquist, 1996] from the perspective of software design. The method for observing the ***trade-offs*** between the design of software and interface metaphor [Yousef, 2001] is needed so that the trade-offs could be regulated. Finally, the seamless ***fusion*** (the integration) of ***form*** (the interface metaphor) and ***function*** (the software) is extremely important [Gaver, 1995]. Poovaiah [1994] has highlighted the need of conceiving the design process of interface as a ***temporal process*** in terms of an interaction across time; as an organization of its various elements. All these issues together indicate that the process for ***visualization*** of interface metaphor needs to be defined. This chapter sets the objectives, defines the scope of work and the limitations of this research. **The dissertation presents a structured process for visualization of interface metaphor. It also shows how the steps of this process are integrated with Software Development Life Cycle (SDLC).**

The important steps of the proposed process are discussed from chapter 3 onwards. **Chapter 3 focuses on how to identify, classify, categorize, assess and then select the *candidate interface metaphors*.** The first section of this chapter brings out how the *candidate interface metaphors* can be identified based on the ***common knowledge dimensions*** of specified users. It explains the ***trilogy*** of knowledge dimensions between the user, the interface metaphor and the software. This section outlines the dimensions of knowledge in terms of ***professional, educational, day-to-day, cultural and miscellaneous***; which help in selecting the *candidate interface metaphors*. If the required knowledge dimension of a *candidate interface metaphor* is not matching with the knowledge available with users then it is rejected.

The second section of chapter 3 provides a technique for identification of *candidate interface metaphors*. It begins by explaining ***unmanifested*** and ***manifested*** states of interface metaphor. In this, ***Commentary of Task Performance (CTP)*** and ***Interface Play Script (IPS)*** are written similar to a drama script. These are juxtaposed and compared to reveal the *candidate interface metaphors*. This technique captures the ***mental model*** of users associated with the tasks taken up for computerization. It mainly captures the ***sensory details*** of the task, which are most essential while visualizing the interface metaphor. These include visual, spatial, verbal, auditory and tactile details familiar to the user. Commentary of Task Performance (CTP) and Interface Play Script (IPS) also provide the *justification* for selecting a particular *candidate interface metaphor*. This technique is more useful for software projects that focus on computerization of existing processes. **It helps in seamless braiding of user's model, user requirements / user experience requirements and design model.**

The third section of chapter 3 shows how the *candidate interface metaphors* can be categorized in terms of **animate** and **inanimate** entities. The *candidate interface metaphors* are classified as **coherent** and **diverse** based on the interrelationships coded in their **cognitive maps**.

The fourth section of chapter 3 shows how the **potential** of an interface metaphor can be assessed based on its conceptual structure. It helps the user interface designer in estimating its **coverage** as against the requirements of software. The *candidate interface metaphors* are further categorized at different **levels** in the **conceptual structure**. These are termed as **Domain, Conglomerate, Multitudinous, Singleton (Animate, Inanimate) conceptual structures** and **Flat concepts.**

Identification, classification, categorization and assessment constitute the sequential steps of the selection process of *candidate interface metaphors*. These are to be performed during the **Requirements Elicitation** stage of software.

Chapter 4 presents various qualitative aspects of interface metaphor and the determinants for tuning and crafting the desired user experiences. The **aspects** of interface metaphor such as **perspective, focus, field of view, flavor, tone, affordances, fusion and multimedia representations** can be tuned to synchronize with the respective **determinants**. The tuning of interface metaphor helps in choosing the right approach for satisfying the **usability objectives** and **user experience requirements** of software. We have termed the **sensation of similarities** between the **reference** and **application domains** as **conceptual resonance.**

Chapter 5 presents a technique for **analyzing** the selected *candidate interface metaphors*. It provides detailed examples of **dissecting** the coherent, diverse and animate interface metaphors. It proves the possibility of dissecting the interface metaphor concept-by-concept; and forming the **Cross-Domain Mappings (CDMs)** between the reference and application domains. Dissection of coherent and diverse interface metaphors reveals their unique characteristics. In case of diverse interface metaphors - the **conceptual proximity and alignment** between **core** and **supporting** metaphors, **cooperative** and **incoherent** integration types are explained. Dissection of an **animate metaphor** shows how the **behavior** of software can be conceptualized on the basis of **traits** and **actions**. This technique is extremely helpful in foreseeing the **missed out** and **hidden software requirements.** It also helps in identifying the skills and efforts required for the design and development of interface metaphor. This chapter introduces new terms like **Unused Concepts (UCs)**, **Unmapped Requirements (URs), Dissection Termination (DT) and Terminus Concept**, which are helpful in interpretation of results. **The dissection of interface metaphor provides objective basis for estimating its coverage and optimization.**

Chapter 6 shows how the **coverage** of *candidate interface metaphors* is **quantified**. It also helps in **measuring the extensibility** of *candidate interface metaphors* for present and future versions of the software. The **quantitative evaluation technique** provides definite parameters for comparing the two or more *candidate interface metaphors*. It also identifies the **weaker traits** of the software from the perspective of animate metaphor for further improvement. The quantitative evaluation also enables the user interface designer in **monitoring and regulating the trade-offs** between the software and interface metaphor. These are mostly in terms of **re-sequencing** and **re-structuring** of software requirements as per the conceptual structure of the interface metaphor. The quantification technique provides several insights into overall conceptual structure of interface metaphor.

Chapter 7 presents a technique for building **User and Application Domain Lexicons**. **Fusion** of **User Domain Lexicon (UDL)** and **Application Domain Lexicon (ADL)** helps in **designing the linguistic metaphors** for user interface.

Formats for building UDL and ADL are designed to integrate unique aspects of domain specific terms and phrases. Special attention is given to context of application and **mental models** associated with the user vocabulary, which helps in revealing the **tacit knowledge** of users. These lexicons are very helpful in not only **reinforcing** the main interface metaphor but also in **capturing the vocabulary of users**. User Domain Lexicon (UDL) can be developed further beyond the scope of a software project.

Chapter 8 provides the **Usability Heuristics of interface metaphor**. We have identified eight major heuristic criteria namely **Familiarity, Representability, Similarity, Extensibility, Compatibility, Co-operability, Cognitive Ergonomics and Feasibility** for **qualitative evaluation** of interface metaphors. Furthermore, there are **23 sub-criteria** and **41 Usability Indicators** identified for ensuring the usability of interface metaphor. The **objective basis** for evaluation is also indicated for each criterion. It is proposed that the **pre-rendering evaluation** of interface metaphor may be performed before taking it up for multimedia rendering. **Quantitative metrics** is also provided for quantifying the results of qualitative evaluation.

Chapter 9 shows how **interactive multimedia** can be used for **design, rendering** and **usability testing** of interface metaphor. **The proposed application of multimedia integrates all the documents and artifacts generated through the visualization process.** It allows the interface designer, software developers and users to **refer, compare, crosscheck** and **corroborate** the linked information. The multimedia rendering of interface metaphor reveals several **hidden software requirements** and **usability problems** related with it. It enables the software designer in **foreseeing the implementation issues**. It can maintain the record of all **evolutionary stages of visualization** along with the **reasons of modifications.** The user interface designer can test the interface metaphor over the specified users and fix the usability problems. Multimedia rendering of interface metaphor can produce several interface components in terms of graphics, layouts, animations, sounds, and the scheme of interaction design. These can be incorporated in the final software. A **remote usability testing** method is also developed for testing the ***cross-cultural*** aspects pertaining to visual representations of interface metaphor. It involves the ***users from diverse geographic locations*** in the testing process.

Chapter 10 shows how the steps of visualization of interface metaphor can be ***integrated and synchronized with SDLC***. It synchronizes the steps of visualization with the steps of ***Requirements Engineering (RE)*** process; such as ***Requirements Elicitation, Analysis*** and ***Specification.*** The visualization process of interface metaphor is to be completed just before the Requirements Specification stage. It helps the software designer in designing the software with adequate understanding of the expected user interface or user experience.

After this the conclusions, the major contributions of this dissertation and future research extensions are documented.

Figure 1.1 on next page presents the structural diagram of the dissertation.

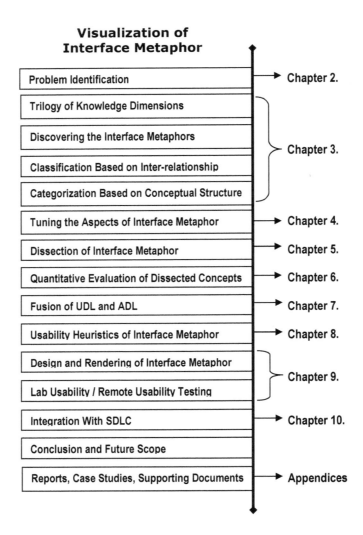

Figure 1.1   Structure of dissertation

Chapter 2. Problem Identification

2.1 Literature Survey

The topic of this dissertation is highly *interdisciplinary* and it touches upon diverse domains such as *Software Engineering, Cognitive Science, Semiotics, Linguistics, Visual Communication and Multimedia Visualization.* This topic of research belongs to the new emerging discipline called *Human-Computer Interaction (HCI)*. It is based on the study of research publications mostly from diverse technical journals and magazines like ACM Interactions and Communications of the ACM, Human Factors in Computing, Man Machine Studies, IEEE Software and SIGGCHI Bulletin. These have regularly covered interdisciplinary articles and papers related to the topic of dissertation. Large number of research papers from the proceedings of international conferences such as Computer Human Interaction (CHI) and HCI International are studied. Most of the journals and conference proceedings were accessed from ACM and IEEE Digital Libraries. The study also includes research papers from a variety of other sources such as Journal of Educational Multimedia and Hypermedia, Journal of Computer Documentation, Journal of Human Computer Studies, etc. There are several other sources like ISO standard for usability and electronic proceedings of a variety of conferences. These are appropriately cited during the deliberations and enlisted in the list of references.

The research papers, articles and books authored / edited by the most notable researchers in the domain of HCI are studied. These include HCI experts like Aaron Marcus, Brenda Laurel, Jakob Nielsen, Thomas Erickson, John Carroll and Keran Holtzblatt. We have also studied the works of George Lakoff (Cognitive Linguist) and Donald Norman (Cognitive Psychologist and Usability Expert). These are appropriately cited while positioning the problem statement of the dissertation.

2.2 State-of-the-art

The research on interface metaphor during 1981–1990 broadly covered its emergence, benefits, understanding of how it works and its applications. Whereas, the later part of research during 1991–2005 raises the problems, issues and gaps in the process of development of interface metaphor. This is a very broad categorization based on prominent trends of the research publications on interface metaphor.

The first Graphical User Interface (GUI) that used menus, buttons, icons and mouse pointer emerged in 1981 from Xerox Palo Alto Research Center (PARC). It was used as part of the 8010 Star Information System designed for business professionals who handled information. Star's GUI represented the typical office environment in the form of Desktop metaphor. The success of Desktop metaphor captured the interest of user interface researchers [Johnson et al., 1989]. This indeed was the beginning of cautious use of metaphor as an integral part of user interface. It proved that interface metaphor could capture the mental model[1] of users [Erickson, 1990]. It inspired further research initiatives on interface metaphor in terms of using the cognitive psychology [Johnson et al., 2000] for improving the effectiveness of user interface.

But the Xerox PARC was not the first to use metaphors. Metaphors have been expressed through language since ages. Metaphors are pervasive in everyday life of humans. We commonly use them for understanding one thing in terms of the other [Lakoff et al., 1980]. If you look at the history, the writings in ancient religious scriptures and iconography are quite metaphorical in nature. *Nyāyasiddhānt Muktāvali* of *Vishwanāthanyāyapanchānan* [17th Century A.D.] provides the definition of metaphor in *Sanskrit* (an ancient Indian language) as below.

तद्भिन्नत्वे सति तद्गतभूयो धर्मवत्त्वम् सादृश्यम् ।

It can be translated as- being different from each other X and Y share many same properties. Humans have always used metaphors as the tool of innovation, creation

---

[1] The gut feeling based on experience used to understand the functionality or behavior of system (Dix et al., 2004).

and communication [Richard, 1941][Gasset, 1925] [Mountford, 2000]. However, the success of Desktop metaphor resulted in several articles and research publications that attempted to define the role, the cognitive model and advantages of using the interface metaphor.

The present understanding of interface metaphor broadly covers following points-

- **It serves as a 'cognitive mediator' [Laurel, 1993] or a 'cognitive ploy' [Palmquist, 1996] for ensuring effective user-system communication [Kass, 1988].**

- **It provides a conceptual model to users for predicting the functionality of a system [Norman, 1988].**

- **It can incorporate the features of real world into the computer application [Nielsen, 1994].**

- **It can help in determining the presentation and behavior of software [Brad, 1990].**

- **It also enables the users to start learning from what is already known and familiar to them [Erickson, 1990].**

- **It superimposes essential similarity (between the software and real world) through visuals (words and images) or through acoustic or tactile means. It also represents the mental models through navigation, tasks and roles [Marcus, 1998].**

With the faster insertion of information technology across the world, usability of user interface became the focal area of research. The trends of research in Human Computer Interaction (HCI) accelerated in the year 1990 [Carroll, 2002]. User interface became a basis for the product's usability and commercial success [Marcus, 1995]. Naturally, the use of interface metaphor is now considered most inevitable [Chen. 2002] aspect of user experience design. **In summary, the interface metaphor continues to be an important area of research in the 21st century [Hamilton, 2000][Marcus, 2002].**

The next section of this chapter identifies the requirements, gaps and problems pertaining to application of interface metaphor in software products.

2.3 Gap Analysis

At the outset of this dissertation, the principal differences between linguistic metaphor and interface metaphor are discussed. Arguments highlighting problems and issues pertaining to interface metaphor are categorized in terms of ***pre-facto analysis, evaluation, design, integration in software*** and ***usability testing.***

2.3.1. Linguistic Metaphor and Interface Metaphor

Traditionally, metaphors were considered to be full sentences and more recently they have been identified in grammatical components, words, phrases, poems and literary passages [Wilcox, 2001]. As per Lakoff et al. [1980] metaphor is part of your thinking and therefore it is expressed through language. Much later, Chandler [1997] has stated that most metaphors are visual at the core. Clair [2000] states that Modern Western European ways of thinking is influenced by print culture that tends to use verbal metaphors; whereas the cultures with oral traditions use visual metaphors. The research performed by cognitive linguists [Moser, 2000] and also the computational linguists [Weiner, 1984] has dominated the prevailing theories of interface metaphor. **As per our observation, linguistic theory is not fully applicable to interface metaphors.** Therefore, linguistic metaphor and interface metaphor are compared in Table 2.1 to bring out their unique characteristics.

| Table 2.1 Comparison of Linguistic Metaphor with Interface Metaphor ||
Linguistic Metaphor	Interface Metaphor
▪ It relies on lexical representations. A word itself is a representation of a concept. Using it metaphorically to map with yet another concept makes it very indirect and complex.	▪ It can be mapped at the conceptual level for shaping the functional and behavioral aspects of interface. It can be represented through visual (static and animated), auditory, spatial, and tactile representations. It is much more direct.
▪ The application is brief, abstract and open to interpretation.	▪ It provides a large conceptual structure.
▪ Major part of the meaning remains implied.	▪ Mostly the concepts within an interface metaphor are cited explicitly.
▪ The application is generally very spontaneous.	▪ The design process needs to be in compliance with the software engineering process. It has to be very methodical.
▪ Linguistic metaphor has a momentary impact. However, the resultant understanding is retained.	▪ The interface metaphor stays with the users for as long as they use the software. The acceptance and

	success of a software product is attributed to its user interface.
▪ It works according to the grammar and rules of language.	▪ No grammar or rules are defined.

This comparison highlights the need of evolving more focused theoretical basis for use of interface metaphors.

2.3.2.   Multi-sensory Experience

The linguistic dependence of metaphoric expressions in olden era was due to lack of multimedia technology. **We can add further to what Lakoff [1980] has said - metaphors in our thought can be manifested through not only language but also through 'visual' and 'audio' media. In addition, the software offers 'interactivity' as another powerful dimension. As per Clair's theory [2000], interface metaphors are more closers to oral cultures that use visual metaphors.** Therefore, metaphoric expressions rendered through multimedia can be far more expressive and experiential.

2.3.3.   Pre-facto Analysis and Evaluation

The **cognitive model**[2] [Norman, 1980] of interface metaphor is primarily based on **post-facto analysis** of software products. There isn't **adequate guidance** available for user interface designers to help in finding suitable interface metaphor [Vaantinen, 1994] [Smilowitz, 1996]. Many interface designers carry out **user trials** [Moll-Carrillo, 1995] on the **randomly chosen interface metaphors**. They face difficulty in selecting a metaphor due to **lack of the theoretical basis** for its **qualitative study** [Madsen, 1994] [Smilowitz, 1996]. **Therefore, the techniques for pre-facto analysis of interface metaphor [Madsen, 1994] are necessary.** The **criteria for evaluation** of metaphor, the method for its **optimization** and **integration** in user interface has to still emerge [Marcus, 1994, 1998] [Vaantinen, 1994]. Also, there is a need to **measure the applicability** and **potential** of a metaphor [Palmquist, 1996] from the perspective of software design. In some situations, multiple metaphors are needed in the same software. The method should guide how **mixed** or **composite** metaphors can be evaluated and applied in the user

---

[2] Cognitive model defines the processes of understanding in humans.

interface [Vaantinen, 1994]. Hudson [2000] while suggesting alternatives to some existing metaphors from the Desktop of Microsoft Windows does not mention the **analysis** of both the existing metaphors and the suggested alternatives. Hedberg [1992] stresses on evaluation of interface metaphors but does not mention how to do it. *These arguments highlight the strong need for evolving a method for pre-facto analysis and evaluation of interface metaphor.*

2.3.4. Design Process

Many times, we have experienced that interface metaphor has influenced the design of software and vice-versa. Interface and software designers have not been able to control this phenomenon. This demands a method for **observing the trade-offs** between the design of software and the interface metaphor [Yousef, 2001] so that they can be **monitored**. Seamless **fusion** of **form** and **function** is extremely important [Gaver, 1995] but it can be achieved only if interface metaphor and software design are integrated during conceptualization. This can be achieved only if the interface metaphor is visualized in the formative stage of software design. If the interface metaphor is introduced after the software is developed then it merely leaves **cosmetic effect** on the interface. This restricts the user interface designer from expressing it effectively. Poovaiah [1994] has also highlighted the need of conceiving the design process of interface as a **temporal process** in terms of an interaction across time; as an organization of its various elements. As stated by Carroll [2002], HCI design will have to be external to the engineering process but the design process has to comply with it for effectiveness of integration with functionality.

Prevailing **software engineering process** [Pressman, 2001] does not provide any defined steps for interface metaphor design. It only makes a general mention of interface design and prototyping. The standard interface guidelines [Apple, 2004], [Microsoft, 2004] do not give coverage to interface metaphors. The Waterfall [Pressman, 2001] or Spiral Models [Boehm, 1988] of SDLC also do not present any defined steps for interface metaphor design. **Therefore, *as computers are moving from professional tools to consumer products, defining a process for design and integration of interface metaphors becomes most essential [Marcus, 1993].***

2.3.5. Testing the Usability

It is observed that some interface metaphors are subjected to varied connotations due to diverse cultural backgrounds of users. Therefore future research needs to explore further the **cultural diversity** of metaphor and its impact on communication [Marcus, 1994] [Duncker, 2002]. No method is defined for ensuring whether one has successfully captured the mental model of users or not. Conducting the usability tests over **geographically distributed locations** and the cost of setting up usability labs are the major prohibitive factors [Redish, 2002]. *This demands a new method and a far-reaching mechanism for the usability testing of interface metaphor.*

2.3.6. Scope and Objectives of Research

Following gaps / research questions pertaining to interface metaphor need to be addressed on priority. Corresponding chapter numbers in the dissertation are indicated in front of each research question, where the solutions are provided.

- How to select the candidate metaphors?   (Chapter 3)
- How to optimize the interface metaphor?   (Chapter 4)
- How to analyze the interface metaphor?   (Chapter 5)
- How to use composite metaphors and evaluate them? (Chapter 3 & 5)
- How to measure the potential of interface metaphor? (Chapter 6)
- How to track the tradeoffs between the design of software and interface metaphor?   (Chapter 6 & Chapter 7)
- How to evaluate the usability of interface metaphor?   (Chapter 8 & Chapter 9)
- How to design the interface metaphor?   (Chapter 9)
- How to synchronize the analysis, evaluation and design of interface metaphor with software engineering process? (Chapter 10)

Analysis, evaluation, design, rendering and usability testing are part of the visualization[3] process of interface metaphor. These steps need to be synchronized with the software engineering process.

---

[3] The term 'visualization' refers with its classical definition, which is as follows: the formation of mental visual images, the act or process of interpreting in visual terms or of putting into visual form. This definition has acquired more meaning in terms of the recall and imagination of all sensory experiences [Owen, 1999].

Following problem statement is derived as an outcome of the discussion so far. It also precisely captures the objective of proposed research.

It is proposed to define a process for visualization of interface metaphor and integrate the steps of this process as part of Software Development Life Cycle (SDLC) to effectively help in crafting the desired user experience.

2.3.6.1.   Limitations of Research

Each of the points summarized while defining the scope can be topics of independent research. However, we propose to define them as steps of entire visualization process of interface metaphor. **Our objective is to facilitate the overall process.**

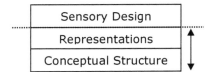

Figure 2.1   Anatomy of Interface Metaphor

As far as possible, we have confined the scope of dissertation to the conceptual structure[4] and the representations of interface metaphor, as both are contiguous and objectively definable. Sensory design is not covered, as there can be infinite design possibilities and subjective opinions about whether it is likable or not. Following are the other limitations of this research-

1. It cannot directly provide the most suitable interface metaphor for the proposed software. But it provides **objective basis** for **classification, categorization, assessment, analysis** and **evaluation** of the interface metaphor.

2. It does not directly provide the proof of correctness while designing the interface metaphor. Proof of correctness can be found only in terms of the acceptance and satisfaction of users. This work provides **Usability Heuristics** for ensuring the correctness (usability) of interface metaphor.

3. The visualization process proposed in this dissertation is applicable for only those software applications, which are meant for common users.

---

[4] Hierarchical organization of abstract ideas

2.4 Choice of Terminology

The linguistic theory of metaphor uses following terminology-

A metaphor consists of two main parts: the **tenor** and the **vehicle** [Richards, 1936]. The tenor is the subject to which the metaphor is applied. The vehicle is the metaphorical term through which the tenor is applied. These two parts come together to reach a point of similarity known as **ground**. For example, a metaphoric statement is given below.

'Senior citizens are like the pillars of our society.'

In the above statement, 'Senior citizens' is the tenor and 'pillar' is the vehicle.

Sanskrit grammar uses following terminology.

उपमेय (*Upameya*) = Tenor   उपमान (*Upamān*) = Vehicle

The semantic relationship between the **tenor** and **vehicle** is generally not explained in the linguistic application of metaphors. It is kept implied and open for interpretation. As shown in table 2.1, the interface metaphor is usually presented in an expanded manner. The similarities are cited quite explicitly throughout the interface. Entire conceptual structure of the interface metaphor (as applicable) is unfolded before the users. **Therefore, we need to use such terminology which can encompass large number of concepts and the multiple structures within the interface metaphor.**

Therefore, we are choosing to call 'tenor' as **application domain**[5] and 'vehicle' as **reference domain**[6]. Also, we will be addressing 'similarities' as **similarities** only. 'Tenor' and 'vehicle' could still be used while discussing a particular similarity between application and reference domains.

Several existing terms are used in the deliberations hereafter. In places where terminology is unavailable, new terms are introduced with proper explanation. The glossary of new terms along with definitions is provided in Appendix M.

---

[5] Application domain is the software for which the user interface is being designed.
[6] Reference domain is the other entity with which the software is being compared.

2.5 Methodology

We have applied both qualitative and quantitative evaluation methodologies (as applicable) while measuring the potential, coverage and usability of interface metaphor. The techniques proposed in this dissertation are used as part of live software projects. Samples of actual user profiles, artifacts, usability tests and reports are documented. The conclusions are substantiated through empirical study, analysis of test results, software artifacts and user feedback. Numerous existing applications of interface metaphors are studied for analysis. Comparisons with the existing knowledge of metaphor are provided wherever applicable for differentiating and highlighting the uniqueness of our work.

Chapter 3. Selection of Interface Metaphor

As discussed in Chapter 2, there is unavailability of adequate guidance for finding suitable interface metaphors [Vaantinen, 1994] [Smilowitz, 1996] and for carrying out its pre-facto analysis [Madsen, 1994]. **In this chapter, we have defined the process for selection of candidate interface metaphors.** It involves following important steps-

- Identification (Explained in section 3.1 and 3.2)
- Classification (Explained in section 3.3)
- Categorization (Explained in section 3.4)
- Assessment of potential (Explained in section 3.4)
- Selection or rejection (Explained through sections 3.1 to 3.4)

3.1 *Identification Based on Common Knowledge*

3.1.1. Dependence on Existing Knowledge

'Find a match between system and the real world', the well-known heuristic of interface design by Nielsen et al. [1990] does not provide any guidance on how to do it. It leaves the interface designer to explore the possible *interface metaphors* all over the world. The real world metaphors invoke the existing knowledge of users. But this idea is not entirely new. As per the ancient Indian *Vedic* literature, metaphors are always conceived out of **Vastu** (entities having existence in our world) [Jha, 1998]. It also mentions that one can create **Avastu** *(non entities)* by combining different objects and properties together. The scope of searching for metaphors in the real world is very vast. As a result, the interface designers have employed **spontaneous / unstructured approach** for exploring the *candidate interface metaphors*. They have been spending a lot of resources on **random exploration** and endless **user trials** [Moll-Carrillo, 1995].

Initially, the software procedures are unknown to the users. In such situation, they are left with no option but to use their existing knowledge for anticipating or guessing the functional behavior of software. But this can happen only if the user interface is designed with appropriate interface metaphors. It offers familiar clues to help in the comprehension of software functionality. The metaphor bridges the gap between the known (existing knowledge) and the unknown (new software procedures). *The discussion so far clearly shows that the cognitive model of interface metaphor mainly depends on the users' existing knowledge. Therefore, defining the existing knowledge of users could indicate the logical direction for exploring the candidate interface metaphors.*

As per Edvinsson et al. [1997], existing knowledge can be categorized in terms of explicit and tacit knowledge. The tacit knowledge is very hard to formalize. *Contrary to spontaneous/ unstructured approach of Hudson [2000] and endless user trials mentioned by Moll-Carrillo [1995], it is preferred to explore the candidate interface metaphors within the specific knowledge dimensions already available with users.*

3.1.2. Trilogy of Knowledge Dimensions

Users accumulate their knowledge from various sources like education, profession, day-to-day life, religion, nature and several miscellaneous activities. This knowledge is applied quite instinctively while deciphering the interface metaphor. As shown in Figure 3.1, any new software demands certain type of pre-requisite knowledge that may or may not be available with users. For example, the schoolteachers are often given multimedia-authoring tools for development of Computer Based Training (CBT) programs. Most of them have adequate expertise in the topic they teach but they may not have any knowledge or skill in using multimedia-authoring tools. This is a universal situation and it requires use of interface metaphors.

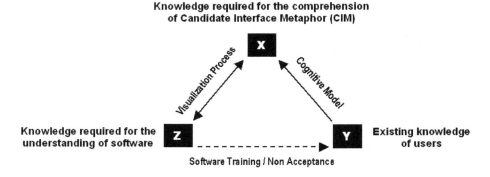

Figure 3.1 Trilogy of Knowledge

The trilogy of knowledge as explained in figure 3.1 shows that at least X and Y coordinates must be matched, as Z may not be under your control. For this purpose it is necessary to identify the Y coordinate well in advance.

3.1.3. Stratification of Users

For a given software project, users must be stratified[7] on the basis of parameters like age, gender, computer awareness, profession, education, economic status, geographic location, culture, etc. Such stratification helps in finding the most common knowledge dimensions among the users. An example is given in Appendix A1.

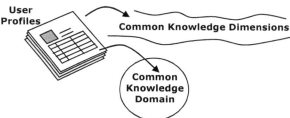

Figure 3.2 User profiling for finding the common knowledge dimensions

3.1.4. Broad Definition of Knowledge Dimensions

Through the study of user profiles, we have broadly defined only five knowledge dimensions as given below. The explicit forms of knowledge are arranged at the top of the list. As you go down the list, it is more of tacit knowledge.

A. Professional

B. Educational

C. Day-to-day

D. Cultural

E. Miscellaneous

Definitions of knowledge dimension and knowledge domain are given below.

- **Knowledge Dimension**

   These are broadly defined sources of users' existing knowledge. Each dimension of knowledge encompasses various knowledge domains.

- **Knowledge Domain**

   It is a well-defined sphere of knowledge.

---

[7] Horizontal status groups of society. Parameters of stratification can be defined as required.

The knowledge dimensions starting from A to D are more relevant for interface metaphor design. All other knowledge domains are clubbed under E, as they are very uncommon and unpredictable.

As shown in Table 3.1, actual data needs to be filled under the column of every knowledge dimension. We have presented the data of three different software projects to show how the most common knowledge dimensions can be identified. The common aspects are underlined.

Table 3.1 Identification of Common Knowledge Dimensions & Domains (Refer the knowledge dimensions indicated as A to E in 3.1.4)					
Projects	**A.**	**B.**	**C.**	**D.**	**E.**
***Dnyaneshwari* CD ROM** [Katre, 1999]	Not possible to define	Different levels of education	* Middle class and above * <u>Knowledge of Marathi Language</u> * <u>Mostly living in Maharashtra state and small proportion of them living in other parts of world</u>	<u>Hindu Marathi culture Maharashtrians</u>	Not possible to define
3D Watershed Game (Appendix A1.)	<u>Professions related to agriculture</u>	Majority of users are illiterate	<u>Rural Maharashtrian Lifestyle</u>	A mix of different religions	Not possible to define
Telemedicine Software	<u>Doctors</u>	<u>Medical Education</u>	Middle class and above	Diverse cultural backgrounds	Not possible to define

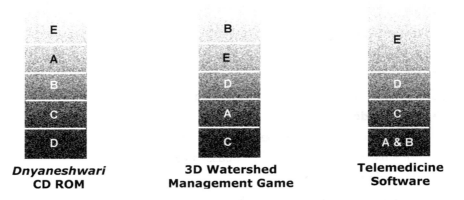

Figure 3.3 Gradation of knowledge dimensions based on commonality

Figure 3.3 shows how the predominance of knowledge dimensions vary depending on the type of users. The dense and darker portion of the vertical stripe conveys the commonality of the knowledge dimension among the stratified users. The gradual dithering of density indicates the non-commonality of the knowledge dimension among the stratified users. For *Dnyaneshwari* CD ROM project, the interface metaphors are chosen from D and C knowledge dimensions. For 3D Watershed game project, the interface metaphors are chosen from C and A dimensions. Original data source of stratification for this project is provided as an example in Appendix A1. For Telemedicine project, the interface metaphors are chosen from A, B and C knowledge dimensions.

3.1.5. Comprehension Based on Knowledge Availability

Each knowledge dimension is briefly explained in the following paragraphs, as the possibility of comprehension of the interface metaphor varies depending on its knowledge dimension. It is indicated in terms of **high, medium** and **low**. Appropriate examples are presented in Appendix A.

Professional and educational knowledge dimensions are discussed together as they are related to each other.

3.1.6. Professional and Educational Dimensions

Users belonging to a stratified group can have similar professional and educational backgrounds. They share common mental models[8] [Johnson-Laird, 1980]. This does not require evidence, as a professional is able to work with different companies operating in the same domain. Persons with similar professional backgrounds from different parts of world can immediately discuss their professional topics. But it is possible that some users may not have educational and professional backgrounds in the same area. Such exceptions may be considered based on their predominance in a stratified group. A detailed example of the cognitive structure based on professional/educational knowledge is presented in Appendix A2.

Examples of interface metaphors with professional and educational knowledge dimensions:

---

[8] The gut feeling based on experience used to understand the functionality or behavior of system [Dix, Finlay, Abowd and Beale, 2004].

Spreadsheet metaphor used in Microsoft Excel software, Desktop metaphor of Macintosh OS, Typewriter metaphor of MS word

Inscript Typing Tutor (Refer Appendix L.) uses 'classroom' interface metaphor as it is designed for school children [Katre, 2005].

The present research documentation nowhere mentions that these metaphors were chosen based on the professional / educational knowledge dimensions. This observation is made during the survey of various applications.

Possibility of comprehension:

Basic terminology, concepts, processes, instruments, materials and hazards of a particular profession are common to professionals like engineers, doctors, architects, designers, etc. It is because they are exposed to standard knowledge through training programs. The fundamentals of a professional domain do not vary. Therefore the possibility of comprehension of interface metaphors based on professional or educational knowledge is *very high*.

3.1.7. Day-to-day Dimension

This type of knowledge is acquired from daily walks of life. The common know-how that we develop as a patient or a bank customer or a passenger or a citizen can be defined and modeled. Though the objectives and processes in common life are similar, the lifestyle is different depending on the geographic and economic conditions. A detailed example of the *cognitive structure* based on day-to-day knowledge is presented in Appendix A3.

Examples of interface metaphors with day-to-day knowledge dimension:

Book metaphor of Adobe Acrobat (refer Table C1 in Appendix C), Mailbox metaphor of e-mail browsers, Planet metaphor of SABRE rely upon day-to-day Knowledge of users.

The appearance of environment and objects differ based on geographic and economic conditions. For example, browser of SABRE (one of the largest Travel

Agency in USA) provides different mailbox icons to account for national differences [Marcus, 1998]. Marcus has presented this case from the viewpoint of cross-cultural acceptability but his paper does not explain about the use of day-to-day knowledge dimension associated with the mailbox metaphor.

Possibility of comprehension:

Day-to-day knowledge may be very superficial but the basic concepts are usually common to a stratified group of users. Everyone is aware of products of day-to-day use but they may not look the same in different geographic regions. Their appearance can be different based on the local taste and prevalence in the specific geographic location. Such interface metaphors generally need to be localized[9] to account for geographic and economic differences. Therefore the possibility of comprehension of interface metaphors based on day-to-day knowledge is at ***medium level***. It can be pushed to high level through ***localization*** of interface metaphor.

3.1.8. Cultural Dimension

Cultural knowledge is very diverse as it depends on traditions, religious, historical and linguistic aspects. Interface metaphors based on cultural knowledge are likely to be misinterpreted or not understood by users from different cultures. User interface designers should be able to isolate such metaphors for testing their cross-cultural applicability. A detailed example is presented in Appendix A4.

There can be a slight overlap between the day-to-day and the cultural knowledge. Day-to-day knowledge should be confined to the activities of daily life. The cultural knowledge may be restricted to religion, traditions, history and language. The boundaries of both knowledge dimensions get diffused in case of illiterate villagers.

Possibility of comprehension:

Interface metaphors with cultural dimension are understandable to a specific community only. Users who belong to another cultures may or may not understand such interface metaphors. Therefore the possibility of comprehension of such

---

[9] Localization pertains to the representation of global technology into particular cultures, local markets or "locales" [Hall, 1997]. This includes the use of local (native) languages, and the design for local customs, beliefs, conventions and practices. [Duncker, 2002].

interface metaphors can be **very high** for a defined set of users; and at the same time it can be **extremely low** for other type of users.

3.1.9. Miscellaneous Dimension

This dimension of knowledge differs from person to person and is highly unpredictable. Miscellaneous knowledge includes domains like hobbies, topics of individual pursuit, etc. It can be useful in rare applications that are designed to address very specialized groups of users.

3.1.10. Reach of Interface Metaphor

Table 3.2 shows the reach of interface metaphor based on each knowledge dimension. The column entitled 'Reach'[10] indicates the applicability of metaphors.

Table 3.2 Reach of Metaphor based on Knowledge Dimensions	
Knowledge Dimensions	**Reach**
A. Professional **B. Educational**	Global users
C. Day-to-day	National or regional level users (Localization as applicable)
D. Cultural	Community specific users
E. Miscellaneous	Special group of users

The reach of metaphor narrows down depending on its knowledge dimension. Table 3.3 shows how the definition of knowledge dimensions has helped in the selection of suitable metaphors.

Table 3.3 Software Projects and Interface Metaphors (Refer the knowledge dimensions indicated as A to E in 3.1.4)			
Software Projects	**Users**	**Knowledge Dimensions**	**Interface Metaphor**
Telemedicine Software	Doctors	A, B and C	Clinic, Operation Theatre, Light box, etc.
QuickMM Album Author [Katre, 2001]	Videographers, Photographers, general users	B and C	Album
JATAN: Virtual Museum Builder [Katre et al., 2004b]	Curators	A, B and C	Museum, register, check approve, publish, withdraw
***Dnyaneshwari* CD Title [Katre, 1999]**	Devotees, Hindu Maharashtrians	C and D	Book and various spiritual metaphors like Lord *Ganesh*, *Gita* Temple

---

[10] Capacity to establish communication with users.

3D Watershed Game	Villagers	C and A	Agriculture, seasons, activities and objects of day-to-day usage in villages
Kumar Vishwakosh (Encyclopedia for School Children)	Students	B and C	Book
Inscript Typing Tutor	Students	B and C	Classroom
Jewelry Accounts and Process Manager	Jewelry shop owner, manager, salesmen, workers, cashiers	A and C	Receipt, Delivery note, collection of cash, order, purchase, etc.

Refer Appendix L. for brief introduction to QuickMM Album Author, JATAN: Virtual Museum Builder, Dnyaneshwari CD Title, 3D Watershed Game, Kumar Vishwa Kosha CD Title and Inscript Typing Tutor.

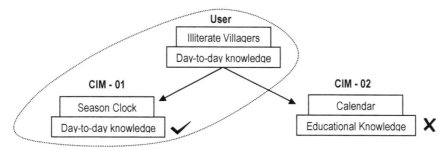

Figure 3.4 Quick evaluation of *Candidate Interface Metaphors (CIM)*

3.1.11. Identification of *Candidate Interface Metaphors*

Matching the knowledge dimensions is extremely helpful in quickly evaluating the suitability of *candidate interface metaphors*. Figure 3.4 shows that season clock can be more easily understandable to villagers than the calendar. The concept behind season clock is explained in Appendix G1.1.

Summary - The stratification and user profiling is helpful in identifying the most common knowledge dimensions of targeted users. Exploration of *candidate interface metaphors* within these knowledge dimensions is more effective than the random approach and endless user trials. The *candidate interface metaphors* can be quickly matched with the knowledge dimensions available with the users to decide the selection.

3.2   Braiding of User's and Design Models

User Centred Design (UCD) *approach recommends detailed study of the user and user domain [Holtzblatt et al., 1995] [Moll-Carrillo, 1995] [Lundell, 1995]. UCD experts have proposed variety of techniques like contextual inquiry [Beyer, 1996] or field study, video documentation of user activities, structured interviewing and participatory design process as general solutions to many usability problems [Dix, et al., 2004]. They have not specified the nature of usability problems that a particular technique can definitely solve. The only thing they unanimously and categorically emphasize is the need of focusing on the user and the centrality of the user in design process. So far no specific technique for identifying the interface metaphors [Vaantinen, 1994] is proposed. Lewis, et al. [1994] in their paper on* **Task Centred User Interface Design** *have also not mentioned about interface metaphors. Brenda Laurel [1993] in her book entitled 'Computer as Theater' does not mention how the interface metaphors can be identified. Moll-Carrillo, Lundell and other UCD theorist seem to have assumed that the metaphor is already found out and straight away one can proceed for user trials. Erickson [2000] and Hudson [2000] have suggested metaphoric options quite spontaneously without mentioning how they arrived at those. Most of the research and experiments seem to have directly started at the metaphor. It is unexplained how did they think of the particular metaphor or what made them notice it?* **Therefore, in this section, a technique is proposed to help the user interface designers in identifying relevant** *candidate interface metaphors* **[Katre, 2005].**

3.2.1.   States of Interface Metaphor

A user interface designer always comes across two different states of interface metaphor namely **unmanifested** and **manifested**. These are explained below.

3.2.1.1.   Unmanifested Metaphor State

In the beginning of a software project, the user interface designer is clueless about which metaphor will be suitable. The software requirements appear vague and are not at all indicative enough. (S)he is stuck up thinking about how to identify the *candidate interface metaphors*. There is a general assumption that the metaphors are always present in the context of application but the user interface designer may not have noticed them. We have termed this particular state of metaphor as the **unmanifested metaphor state**.

3.2.1.2. Manifested Metaphor State

In some situations, the user interface designer quickly gets an idea of possible *candidate interface metaphors*. At times, (s)he foresees the *candidate interface metaphors* even before starting to elicit the software requirements. At times, the customer brief explicitly suggests the desired interface metaphor. We have termed this state of metaphor as the **manifested metaphor state**. It means one does not require to find the *candidate interface metaphors*.

The transition of *candidate interface metaphors* from *unmanifested* to *manifested* state needs to be defined. How does it happen? And what makes it happen? Usually the ability of identifying the suitable interface metaphor is attributed as insight, talent and creativity of the interface designer. But HCI practitioners need a definite technique for this purpose.

3.2.2. Technique for Identification of *Candidate Interface Metaphors*

Therefore, it is proposed to write the **Commentary of Task Performance (CTP)** and **Interface Play Script (IPS)** for identification of *candidate interface metaphors*. **This technique should not be mixed with Use Cases [Schneider et al., 1999] or Cognitive Walkthrough [Polson et al., 1992] as it has entirely different objectives. The comparative observations are presented in 3.2.3.**

3.2.2.1. General Guidelines

- Both Commentary of Task Performance (CTP) and Interface Play Script (IPS) have to be written in the manner of a typical drama script. The script is divided on the basis of 'tasks' similar to 'scenes' in a drama script.
- **The main focus of documentation should be on detailing the experiential factors of the task being performed. It includes sensory details in terms of visual, spatial, verbal, auditory and tactile which are most familiar to the user.**
- One of the objectives of this activity is to capture the mental model of users.
- In place of 'character names', one has to mention the participants involved in a task e.g. operator, director, manager, salesman, etc. The list of participants of a task, description of the situation and assumptions have to be

documented before starting to write Commentary of Task Performance (CTP) and Interface Play Script (IPS).

- The language of writing should be simple and straightforward.
- Having finished the documentation of Commentary of Task Performance (CTP) and Interface Play Script (IPS), both should be juxtaposed for identifying the *unmanifested* metaphors.

3.2.2.2. Commentary of Task Performance (CTP)

Writing the Commentary of Task Performance (CTP) involves following steps-

- Focus on **conventional processes** in the user environment.
- Observe the selected tasks performed by the targeted users. These tasks should be the ones that are expected to be computerized. User interface designer has to repeatedly observe each task performance until the **common pattern** and flow of activities become evident.
- It should mention all the objects (important as well as trivial) used for completing the task and the purpose for which they were used. The **sensory clues** in terms of **visual, spatial, verbal, auditory** and **tactile** details should be documented. Users need these clues for predicting the status of a task.
- The commentary of such task performances by the users should be documented in the **narrative form**. It should include the details of situations, options, goals, actions, decisions and the outcome.
- It should also include the documentation of **significant interruptions, dependencies** and **constraining factors** faced while performing the task.

3.2.2.3. Interface Play Script (IPS)

Preparation of Interface Play Script (IPS) involves following steps-

- User interface designer should now visualize how the user would perform the same task using the proposed software.
- The visualization should be documented in terms of user inputs and system response.
- The documentation may include general details of user interface. There is no need to stretch your imagination to mention component level details of user interface.
- Source of user input (background work) should also be specified.

3.2.3. Comparison with Cognitive Walkthrough

Polson et al. [1992] to evaluate the user interface reintroduced cognitive walkthrough approach, which was originally used for evaluation of code in software engineering. In this approach, the evaluator steps through every action that user will perform for achieving a goal. In Cognitive Walkthrough, the objective is to check the actions, user goals, communication of actions and feedback. This method is to be used after the prototyping stage [Dix et al., 2004]. It focuses on identifying the probable usability problems.

Table 3.4 shows the principal differences between the Cognitive Walkthrough and the technique proposed by us in this section.

Table 3.4 Comparison of Cognitive Walkthrough with IPS and CTP	
Cognitive Walkthrough	**IPS and CTP**
▪ Action sequence is restricted within the software domain.	▪ Action sequences are from both physical and software domains.
▪ Focus is on the technical description of actions, user interface and goals [Rieman et al., 1995]	▪ Attention is on the context, situations, objects, human roles, sensory clues involved in the task.
▪ The purpose is to verify the source code or user interface action sequence.	▪ The main purpose is to captures users' mental model
▪ It is an evaluation method.	▪ It is a visualization method.
▪ Objective is to find gaps and problems.	▪ Objective is to find the *candidate interface metaphors*.

Above comparison conclusively highlights how the Cognitive Walkthrough and the technique proposed in this section are different. Researchers are very likely to compare it with Use Cases as it uses the terminology of 'actors'. But the prime objective of Use Case Modeling is to define the system functionality in Object Oriented software development [Schneider et al., 1999]. The technical report of Usability Throughout SDLC: A Summary of Interact 2001 Workshop prepared by Jan Gulliksen et al. concludes the debate on Use Case versus Task Analysis, which categorically mentions that Use Case Modeling does not address the usability requirements. They demand for greater amount of detailing from the viewpoint of user interface designers.

During the development of Virtual Museum Builder we faced the *unmanifested metaphor state*. The proposed method was used for identification of *candidate interface metaphors*. The format used for documentation of Commentary of Task Performance (CTP) and Interface Play Script (IPS) is shown in Table 3.5.

Table 3.5 Juxtaposing CTP and IPS	
Task 1. Creation of a museum record	
Participants: Data Entry Operator, Curator, Curatorial Assistant, Director, Office Boy	
Assumptions:	
The Data Entry Operator, Curator and Director are always looking through the web browsers and waiting for change in the status of a given record. They know the result of setting a particular flag.	

	Commentary of Task Performance	**Interface Play Script**
1.	**Curator:** Prepares the draft records by writing them on separate sheets. He refers books, consults experts and finishes the draft version.	**Curator:** Prepares a hand written record of an artifact and gives it to the Data Entry Operator. *(Either he delivers it himself or asks the office boy to hand it over)*
2.		**Data Entry Operator:** On receiving the hand written record, he clicks on new record button in the Integration Module of VMB.
3.		**Software:** Provides a new form for data entry.
4.		**Data Entry Operator:** Clicks the browse button for selection of relevant images.
5.		**Software:** A typical file browser window appears on the screen with thumbnail images.
6.	**Curator:** Provides a photograph or a transparency from the catalogs maintained by museum. He uses a light box for viewing the transparencies.	**Data Entry Operator:** Selects the image by matching the accession no. of a record with the image file name. Confirms the digitized image by tallying it with the transparency. On finishing the data entry he sets the flag as 'Finished'. If the data entry is incomplete, he sets the flag as 'Unfinished'. An unfinished record is not forwarded to Curator.
7.		**Software:** On setting the flag as 'Finished' the software flashes a message that 'The finished record is now forwarded to Curator for verification.' (A 'finished' record is read only.)
8.		**Curator:** Checks the record, comments it if it has

		typographic errors and sets the flag as 'Commented'. (A commented record is editable.)
9.		**Data Entry Operator:** Reads the comment. Opens the record. Corrects the typing errors and then sets the flag as 'revised'.
10.		**Software:** Flashes a message that the revised record is forwarded to Curator for verification.
11.		**Curator:** Opens the record. Checks the revised record and sets the flag as 'checked'. (A checked record is read only.)
12.	**Curator:** The handwritten record is forwarded to the Director of museum in an envelope / folder with a covering note requesting his approval. (Covering note is dated and signed).	**Software:** Flashes a message that the checked record is now forwarded to Director for approval.
13.	**Office Boy:** Picks up the envelope/folder and delivers it to the Director. (Keeps it in the In Tray of Director)	
14.	**Director:** Writes / makes corrections in the draft records, signs, puts the date and then marks the folder / envelope back to Curator. Uses red/ green colored ink pen for writing. The envelope/folder is kept in the Out Tray.	**Director:** Finds a Checked record submitted for approval. He verifies the contents and in case of correction 'Comments' it.
15.	**Office Boy:** Picks up the envelope/folder and delivers it to the Curator. It is kept in the In Tray of Curator.	
16.	**Curator:** Opens the folder and finds Director's comments for corrections.	**Curator & Data Entry Operator:** Work towards improving the record as instructed by the Director and set the flag as 'Finalized'.
17.	**Curator:** Incorporates the corrections (rewrites it) and submits it again by placing his signature and date to Director for approval.	**Software:** Flashes a message that the Finalized record is now forwarded to Director for approval.
18.	**Director:**	**Director:**

	Approves it (places his signature and date) and returns it to Curator.	Verifies the contents of finalized record and checks the history of comments so far. Sets the flag to 'Approved'.
19.	**Curatorial Assistant:** Enters it in the Main Accession Register.	The approved record is automatically added in the Main Accession Register.

It is possible to detail a particular step further in a similar manner. For example, the sample commentary presented in Table 3.5 does not provide enough details of manual record preparation and the data entry using proposed software. User interface designer can decide to write elaborate commentary of the sub-tasks.

3.2.3.1. *Candidate Interface Metaphors* Identified

1. It was possible to identify the *candidate interface metaphor* like 'In and Out Trays' in the offices of Curator and Director (Steps 13. and 15.). They are used for representing the received and forwarded records in VMB software. Appendix B1 explains this example in greater details.

2. Many steps in Commentary of Task Performance (CTP) show that the task is ending up with a register entry (Step 19.). 'Register' is the most commonly used term in Indian museums. The museums have variety of registers like gallery, section, store, loan, conservancy, main accession, etc. 'Register' metaphor is used in VMB software for representing various modules like Data Entry, Administration, Subscription, Main Accession, etc.

3. We have introduced a concept of 'Image Catalog' for arranging the preview of digitized images (Step 6.). Light box is also a *candidate interface metaphors*.

4. Every time, the Curator and Director place their signatures with dates after recording their decisions (Steps 12. and 18). In VMB software, a record becomes 'Read Only' for the sender after (s)he comments and forwards it. The history of comments shows all transactions with dates and timings.

5. 'Closed and open envelopes' are used with unique markings to indicate the status of a record (Steps 12. to 15.). Each record has a flag indicating its

status such as finished, revised, checked, commented, approved, published, withdrawn, etc.

6. Different ink colors are used for presenting the comments of Curator and Director (Step 14.).

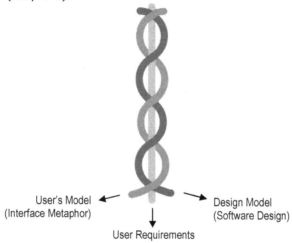

Figure 3.5 The braiding of user's model with design model

Figure 3.5 shows how the technique of Commentary of Task Performance (CTP) and Interface Play Script (IPS) helps in braiding the user's model with design model. The intuitive and spontaneous approach of using interface metaphor does not braid properly.

Summary - Juxtaposing of Commentary of Task Performance (CTP) and Interface Play Script (IPS) is helpful in identifying the *candidate interface metaphors*. This method captures the user's mental model associated with the tasks taken up for computerization. It mainly captures the sensory details of the task, which are essential for interface design. It includes visual, spatial, verbal, auditory and tactile details familiar to the user. Commentary of Task Performance (CTP) and Interface Play Script (IPS) also provide the justification for selecting a particular interface metaphor. This technique is more applicable for such software projects that are intended to computerize existing processes.

3.3 Classification Based on Interrelationships

Having identified the *candidate interface metaphors*, as discussed in earlier sections, the interface designer has to now classify them. We have proposed new classes based on the *interrelationships* between the *candidate interface metaphors*. These classes are named as *coherent* and *diverse* metaphors. The reasons of defining these new classes are discussed below.

*Researchers have used the terms like **mix metaphors** [Vaantinen, 1994] or **composite metaphors** [Carroll, 1988] [Smilowitz, 1996] interchangeably to convey the usage of multiple metaphors in combination for representing the structure of software. Another term called **integral metaphor** is used as the opposite of composite metaphors [Smilowitz, 1996]. An interface metaphor is always a mix or a composite of multiple metaphoric concepts. The thesaurus [Roget's Thesaurus, 1990] presents **integral and composite as synonyms** of each other. The use of such overlapping and ambiguous terms is due to lack of clarity about the footing on which the metaphors are differentiated. These terms appear to be loosely defined as the researchers intended only to describe or characterize the particular phenomenon of interface metaphors. They have not stated any specific differentiators for **classification** of candidate interface metaphors.*

One realizes that some of the *candidate interface metaphors* can be grouped together due to common attributes. At the same time some *candidate interface metaphors* or groups of *candidate interface metaphors* remain isolated. Basically, the metaphors, which get grouped together, have correspondence with our ***cognitive map***[11] [Kearney et al., 1997]. The isolated ones are disconnected from the cognitive map or they originate from different cognitive maps and therefore they stand apart.

We are essentially pointing towards the interrelationship between the *candidate interface metaphors*. This interrelation can be established on the basis of following points.

- Are they originating from same source?
- Are they logical part of same workflow or activity?

---

[11] Cognitive maps are a particular kind of representation of mental model that represent important objects and concepts, and code the relationships among them.

- Are they conceptually connected?
- Are they part of the cognitive map of specified users?

All four points mentioned above define the coherence between *candidate interface metaphors*.

3.3.1. Coherent Interface Metaphors

Characteristics of coherent interface metaphors are as under-

- They are part of the same cognitive map.
- They can be recalled, guessed or logically inferred by the user.
- They belong to same or related knowledge dimensions and domains.
- They originate from same source.
- They are logical parts of same activity or a workflow.
- They are conceptually connected.
- Coherent metaphors emerge if the software is addressing one type of problems and targeted at single type of users.
- They can be coherent metaphors even if they comply any one or more or all characteristics mentioned above.

Example:

If you take the desktop metaphor: files, folders, calculator, printer, diary, trash can, etc. are the objects that are found around the desktop in an office environment. They are also used in the office activities. This itself is the common interrelation they all share with each other. Users' can exactly recall these objects from the office environment, as they are coherent and part of single cognitive map. Even if the desktop example is very over exposed, the 'coherent' aspect is not stated anywhere. While mentioning the integral metaphors, Smilowitz [1996] is actually highlighting the *coherence* between the metaphorical concepts.

3.3.2. Diverse Interface Metaphors

Researchers have been referring the quality of diversity while mentioning mix or composite metaphors.

Characteristics of diverse interface metaphors are as under-

- They are not part of single cognitive map.
- They cannot be recalled, guessed or logically inferred by the user. They appear before the user in an unexpected way.
- They belong to unrelated knowledge dimensions and domains.
- They originate from diverse sources.

- They are not logical parts of same activity or a workflow.

- They are conceptually unrelated or disconnected.

- Diverse metaphors are required when the software is addressing diverse types of problems and multiple types of users. The root of diverseness of interface metaphors can be found in the software scope.

Example:

The QuickMM Album Author software [Katre, 2001] uses Album, Exhibition, Portfolio, Catalog, Calendar, and Greeting Card metaphors. They have no relation with each other. Users can't recall them together as they are not part of common activity or workflow or cognitive map.

Dealing with coherent metaphors is relatively simpler. But with diverse metaphors, mismatches can emerge due to conceptual overlapping. The classification of metaphors can help the designer notice the possible overlaps in the early stage. The diverse metaphors, in many scenarios, can also help in producing magical features (This aspect is further elaborated in 4.1.5). They can help in combining the seemingly unrelated attributes together in software.

Summary - The *candidate interface metaphors* can be classified based on their *interrelationships* as *coherent* and *diverse* interface metaphors. Coherent interface metaphors are part of single cognitive map unlike the diverse metaphors that belong to different and unconnected cognitive maps. This type of classification provides basis for the selection process.

3.4 Assessment Based on Conceptual Structure

The earlier section has shown, how the *candidate interface metaphors* are classified based on their interrelationship. Furthermore, in this section, we have proposed new categories based on different levels of the conceptual structure such as *Domain, Conglomerate, Multitudinous, Singleton (Inanimate, Animate)* and *Flat concept*. These signify different levels of underlying conceptual structure. The reasons behind forming such categories are discussed below.

There is insufficient guidance available to help the user interface designers in finding suitable interface metaphors [Vaantinen, 1994], [Madsen, 1994], [Smilowitz, 1996]. As a result, many of them seem to be using metaphors with little understanding of its underlying structure [Barr, 2002]. They are also seen using linguistic categories of metaphor and taxonomies [Barr, 2002] in interface design such as metonymy [Marcus, 1993] ontological, personification, orientational and structural [Barr, 2002]. These categories mainly signify the style of application or a particular type of metaphor. These are not intended to signify anything about the levels within the conceptual structure. In case of interface metaphors, it is extremely important to know different levels within the conceptual structure for the quick assessment of its potential.

The 'desktop' of Macintosh OS is treated as an organizational metaphor [Vaantinen, 1994] but it does not indicate anything about its conceptual structure. The same type is referred as structural [Marcus, 1998] [Barr, 2002] or organizational [Vaantinen, 1994] interchangeably. The terms 'structural or organizational metaphor' also do not signify anything about the potential of conceptual structure. Judge [1991] has already mentioned about the need to define the characteristics of conceptual structures. However, *we are not advocating against using the categories of linguistic metaphors in interface design.*

The reference domain can be fragmented into worlds, environments, objects and elements. These fragments have an inherent hierarchy as shown in Figure 3.6. The hierarchical fragments of a domain provide the basis for defining various levels of conceptual structure.

The levels within the conceptual structure of reference domain are indicated below.

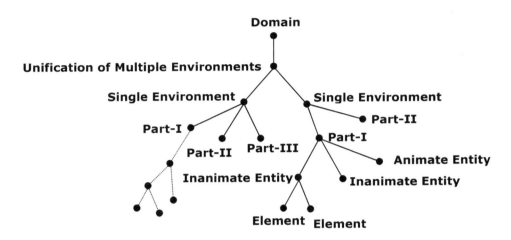

Figure 3.6 The conceptual structure of a domain

3.4.1.   Animate and Inanimate Metaphors

A domain comprises of animate and inanimate entities. Such entities are applicable as animate and inanimate metaphors. But both of them have *Singleton* conceptual structures.

3.4.1.1.   Inanimate Metaphor

This type of candidate interface metaphor represents the inanimate entity (objects) from the users' work environment. **Such inanimate entities are called as *inanimate metaphors.*** It is possible to conceptualize certain functionalities of software based on *inanimate metaphors*, e.g., Book, Album, Diary, Register/Catalog, Spread Sheet, Typewriter, etc.

3.4.1.2.   Animate Metaphor

This type of candidate interface metaphor represents the animate entity (humans) from the users' work environment. **Such animate entities are called as *animate metaphors.*** While observing the users' work environment, you not only come across inanimate entities but also animate entities like humans playing the designated roles such as Accountant, Teacher, Assistant, Secretary,

Adviser, Curator, Manager, etc. It is possible to conceptualize the behavior of software based on *inanimate metaphors.*

3.4.2. Levels of Conceptual Structure

Different hierarchical levels in the conceptual structure as shown in Figure 3.6 have been named to indicate their potential. It is obvious that a domain provides the richest conceptual structure and levels below are relatively less richer.

Domain	-	*Domain*
Unification of Multiple Environments	-	*Conglomerate*
Single Environment	-	*Multitudinous*
Animate Entity	-	*Singleton*
Inanimate Entity	-	*Singleton*
Element /Superficial application	-	*Flat concept*

3.4.2.1. Domain

A domain is basically a large sphere of activities, which provides a very complex and rich conceptual structure. It can hold several groups of environments together, e.g., the city metaphor chosen by Dieberger [1998] for visualization of large volume of information, provides a ***domain conceptual structure.*** But his paper does not define the levels of conceptual structures. The *domain conceptual structure* can contain several *conglomerate conceptual structures.*

3.4.2.2. Conglomerate

It is a conceptual structure of such interface metaphor that integrates several environments or groups of conceptual structures together. For example, the 'university' metaphor has a ***conglomerate conceptual structure***. A university is made up of several departments. A *conglomerate conceptual structure* can contain several *multitudinous conceptual structures.*

3.4.2.3. Multitudinous

The user interface designer can select an environment that includes multiple entities (animate and inanimate), e.g., Desktop, Library, Gallery, Office Cabin, Classroom, Doctor's Clinic, Studio, etc. Such metaphoric environments provide multitudinous conceptual structures. It can integrate a variety of *conceptual structures* like *multitudinous, inanimate singleton, animate singleton* and *flat concepts* as shown in Figure 3.7. The concepts within a *multitudinous conceptual structure* are generally coherent.

3.4.2.4. Singleton

Both animate and inanimate metaphors have *singleton conceptual structures*. **It is a single hierarchy of concepts.** There can be many *inanimate and animate singleton conceptual structures* as part of a *multitudinous conceptual structure*.

3.4.2.5. Flat Concept

The concept at the terminus of a branch within the conceptual structure is called as flat concept. In some software products, even the *domain, conglomerate and multitudinous conceptual structures* are applied very superficially. These are grossly underutilized in the given circumstances. Such application of interface metaphor can be referred as *flat concept(s)*. Well-known examples of *flat concepts* are Eraser, Scissor and Paste tools in MS Word or exhibition metaphor in Album Author [Katre, 2001].

Usually any conceptual structure of interface metaphor has large number of *flat concepts*. They can be part of either any of the conceptual structures or they can even exist without any relationship with other metaphors.

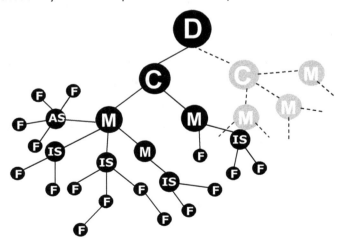

Domain (D), Conglomerate (C), Multitudinous (M), Inanimate Singleton (IS),
Animate Singleton (As) and Flat (F) Concept.

Figure 3.7 Visual representation of conceptual structure

3.4.3. Assessment Based on Conceptual Structure

The assessment based on conceptual structure of interface metaphor helps the user interface designer in visualizing the suitability of a *candidate interface metaphor* vis-à-vis the requirements of software. It is possible to draw following inferences as a result of this assessment. These inferences are further substantiated in Chapter 6.

1. If there is large number of *flat concepts* in any of the conceptual structures then –

   ▪ It is unable to cover the clusters of functionalities.

   ▪ The interface metaphor is applied at skin level.

   ▪ If the interface design activity is initiated after the software is developed then most of the time you end up with *flat concepts* only.

2. If there is greater number of *singleton conceptual structures* then-

   ▪ The conceptual mappings seep deeper into the software.

   ▪ Users can figure out the functionality of software with intuition.

3. If it is a *domain or conglomerate conceptual structure* then it is bound to have adequate number of *multitudinous, singleton conceptual structures* and *flat concepts*. In such case -

   ▪ The user interface has potential to emerge as one of the prominent selling points of the software. It also means that if you fail to capitalize on this potential then your competitor might do it for a similar software product.

   ▪ Analysis, evaluation, design and testing of such interface metaphor are going to be very demanding. Sufficient provision of resources in terms of skills, efforts and finance must be anticipated in the project.

   ▪ There can be adequate potential for covering the future versions of software.

Discussion

This chapter has shown how the knowledge dimensions of metaphor and the user need to be matched for proper understanding of the interface metaphor. The standard table indicating the reach of interface metaphors based on knowledge dimensions is extremely handy for quick reference. We could also see how the *candidate interface metaphors* could be identified by juxtaposing the Commentary of Task Performance (CTP) and Interface Play Script (IPS). In this, greater emphasis is given on capturing the mental model of users and sensory details, which are essential for interface design. After this, the *candidate interface metaphors* are classified on the basis of their interrelations in terms of *coherent* and *diverse* classes. This classification highlights the role of cognitive maps in guessing or anticipating software functionality.

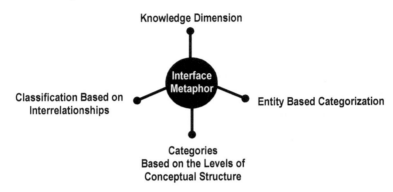

Figure 3.8 Primary attributes of interface metaphor

Then the *candidate interface metaphors* are categorized based on different levels of conceptual structure through newly defined categories like *domain, conglomerate, multitudinous, singleton (animate, inanimate)* and *flat concepts.* This type of categorization helps in judging the potential of the *candidate interface metaphors.* Sample template used for the selection of *candidate interface metaphors* is given in Table 3.6.

Table 3.6 Template for Selection Process	
Project	Digital collection management system for museums
Users	Museum staff
Most Common Knowledge Dimensions	Professional and day-to-day
Knowledge Domain	Archeology, Museology
Reach	Global
Localization	Very small percentage
Juxtaposing of CTP and IPS	Done (Results given below)
Candidate Interface Metaphors	**Museum** (Gallery, Exhibits, Register, Records, In/Out tray, Catalog, Light Box, etc.)
Knowledge Dimensions of Metaphor	A mix of professional and day-to-day
Matching of Knowledge Dimensions	Positive
Possibility of Comprehension	High
Relational Classification	Coherent
Structural Category	Museum- *Conglomerate* Gallery- *Multitudinous*

	Other- *Inanimate Singleton*
Potential of Interface Metaphor	High
Decision	**Selected**

Summary - It is possible to perform the selection process in parallel with the requirements elicitation activities as part of SDLC (refer chapter 10). This method provides an objective basis for selection of interface metaphors unlike the random or spontaneous approaches practiced by the interface designers.

Chapter 4. Tuning the Interface Metaphor

After selecting the *candidate interface metaphors as specified in earlier chapter*, we require to tune them for the given software project. In this chapter, we have identified the *aspects* and the respective *determinants* of interface metaphor, which need to be tuned for crafting the desired user experience.

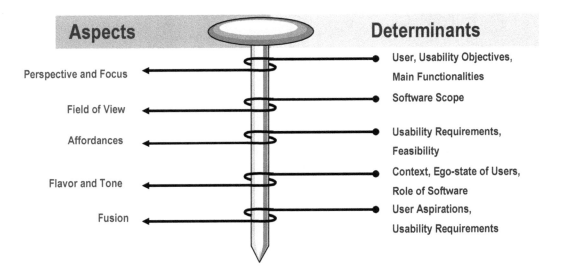

Figure 4.1 Aspects of interface metaphor and the determinants for tuning the user experience

It is well known that the same interface metaphor can project different images, highlight different similarities and offer different quality of experiences [Madsen, 2000] depending on its tuning. Some researchers have called this phenomenon as illusion or magic [Marchak, 2000], [Madsen, 2000]. There have not been adequate efforts to define the nature of this variance. **A special study to find the variant aspects of interface metaphor and the determinants of its variance is performed (refer Appendix C.).** The findings of this study are discussed hereafter.

4.1 Aspects and Determinants for Tuning the User Experience

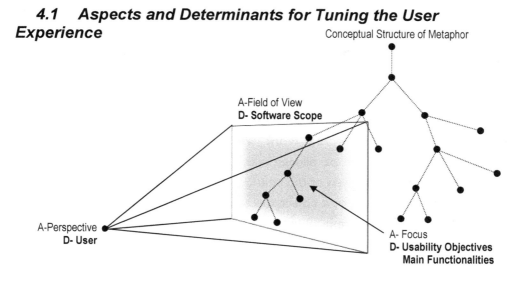

Aspect (A), Determinants (D)

Figure 4.2 Perspective, Focus and Field of View

The determinants are mentioned under each aspect.

4.1.1. Perspective and Focus

▪ **Perspective**

Perspective means the position from which the user interface designer views at the reference object or domain, used as an interface metaphor. Of course the user interface designer has to align his perspective to that of the user.

▪ **Focus**

The focus decides the amount of detailing and prominence given to certain metaphoric concepts. It keeps irrelevant concepts out of its focus. The perspective and focus of interface metaphor can be decided based on the user, the usability objectives and the main functionalities of software.

The reference domain along with its hierarchy of environments, objects and elements can be mapped with the software as interface metaphors. These are treated as concepts. Even if certain objects and elements of a reference domain are visible in reality, it does not mean that each of them will be sharply defined and given prominence in the overall composition of interface metaphor at all times. Similar to the camera lens, the user interface designer can keep only certain aspects of interface metaphor in focus and the rest out of its focus. Refer Appendix C1.1 for examples.

The determinants of *perspective* and *focus* namely *user, usability objectives* and *main functionalities* are given below.

- **User**

User is someone who does 'real work' with the computer. The perspective of interface metaphor needs to be aligned with the perspective of users. It helps in capturing the most familiar view of the interface metaphor. Users with varied profiles are not exposed to the referred object the same way. Their view of the reference object is likely to be different. What they notice and what they ignore in the reference object depends on their perspective. User profiling and contextual study [Holtzblatt, 1995] can help in understanding the perspective of users.

- **Usability Objectives**

Usability objectives define explicit usability goals in terms of *learnability, flexibility* and *robustness* of the software product from the user's point of view. The other principles that affect the learnability of software are ***predictability, synthesizability, familiarity, generizability*** and ***consistency*** [Dix et al., 2004]. The usability objectives primarily focus on 'quality in use' [ISO/IEC FDIS 9126-1, 2000]. The interface metaphor significantly contributes towards improving the usability of software.

- **Main Functionalities**

Main and mundane functionalities of software are outlined during the decomposition or elaboration of problems. The main functionalities that are must to be delivered get outlined while software scoping is done [Pressman, 2001]. However, the degree of importance given to them can defer.

It is obvious that if the interface metaphor is not contributing to achieving the usability objectives then it is serving no purpose. Similarly, if it is ignoring the most important functionalities of software (which also translates into the main problems to be addressed by the software) then also it has no use.

The concepts within the interface metaphor resulting in conceptual resonance[12] with the main functionalities of software must be kept in focus.

We can summarize that the users, the usability objectives and the main functionalities of proposed software determine the 'perspective' and 'focus' of interface metaphor.

4.1.2. Field of View

Field of view means an enclosing border of visibility. The field decides how much portion of the scene to be permitted in the view. Similarly, user interface designer has to decide which portion of the interface metaphor to be kept in the view or out of the view. Refer Appendix C1.2 for examples.

The *field of view* is determined by the *software scope*, which is defined below.

- **Software Scope**

Software scope describes the data and control to be processed, function, performance, constraints, interfaces, and reliability [Pressman, 2001]. More importantly the boundaries of the scope need to be considered while setting the field of view for interface metaphor.

The field of view of interface metaphor can be determined based on the scope of -

- software or
- a particular module of software or
- a cluster of functionalities

This depends on how much portion of software the interface metaphor is intended to cover.

4.1.3. Affordances

Affordance of the interface metaphor means, the perceived and actual properties of the thing, primarily those fundamental properties that determine just how the thing could properly be used [Norman, 1990 and 1999]. Wood et al. [2004] suggest to incorporate the physical and social affordances. We would like to consider even the interactive, behavioral and cognitive affordances in the context of interface metaphors. The affordances of an interface

---

[12] Re-echoing of concepts due to similarity between the source and the target in a metaphoric application.

metaphor are incorporated in order to satisfy the usability requirements. But it also depends on technical feasibility. Refer Appendix C1.3 for examples.

The determinants for *affordances* namely *usability requirements* and *feasibility* are given below.

- **Usability Requirements**

Usability requirements define the capability of the software product to be understood, learned, used and attractive to the user, when used under specified conditions [ISO/IEC FDIS 9126-1, 2000].

- **Feasibility**

The feasibility of incorporating all the selected affordances of interface metaphor involves technical and resource (time, skills, finance) feasibility [Pressman, 2001]. Depending on the feasibility constraints the affordances of interface metaphor are chosen for development.

The affordances of interface metaphor are determined on the basis of whether they help in meeting the usability requirements and the feasibility constraints.

4.1.4. Flavor and Tone

- **Flavor**

Flavor provides appropriate (familiar) taste of the content to users. Toms et al [1999] have referred the 'genre' as interface metaphor, which has some similarity with flavor. User interface designer has to choose appropriate representations from the overall context of software for rendering the interface metaphor with right flavor.

- **Tone**

Tonal quality of sound can be decided in terms of its pitch and strength. Whereas, the tonal quality of a picture can be decided in terms of light and shade. Similarly, the tonality of presentation of interface metaphor can be tuned for satisfying the ego-state of users and the role to be played by the software.

Both flavor and tone can be tuned in terms of representations, shapes, colors, layouts, sounds and the interaction design to offer a certain quality of experience to users. Refer Appendix C1.4 for examples.

The determinants for *flavor* and *tone* namely *context, ego state of users* and *role of software* are given below.

- **Context**

The context provides detailed information about user domain, work environment, psychological aspects and other preferences emerging out of social and cultural context [Holtzblatt, 1995].

- **Ego State of Users**

A consistent pattern of thinking, feeling and experience directly related to a corresponding consistent pattern of behavior [Berne, 1961].

- **Role of Software**

Refer the discussion on *animate metaphor* in 3.4.1 for explanation on role of software.

4.1.5.   Fusion

Fusion involves combining real life affordances of the reference object with the software. These can be partly helpful in offering real world experience to users.

Affordances of two or more reference objects can also be fused together to overcome certain constraints, which are faced in real life. These can be called as magical super-affordances. The fusion has to be carried out in successive steps. It begins with the known and then goes beyond it. The terminus[13] defines the threshold for crossing over the constraints. Interface metaphors can be helpful in innovating by combining the affordnaces of different objects together or by adding entirely new (innovative) or magical affordances. The metaphor evokes existing mental model [Johnson-Laird, 1980] of users and then goes beyond it as a surprise. The software overcomes the

---

[13] Terminus is the endpoint of decomposing the branch of a conceptual structure, preferred by interface designer.

constraints and difficulties of real life by producing a magical effect in user's mind. This fusion can be tuned to address the aspirations of users. Refer Appendix C1.5 for examples.

The determinants of this *fusion* namely *user aspirations* and *usability requirements* are given below.

- **User Aspirations**

User aspirations can be defined in terms of their needs, motivations, goals and constraining factors. The context study provides information on user aspirations.

- **Usability Requirements**

Usability requirements as mentioned in 4.1.3 and user aspirations both help in determining how the fusion of interface metaphor and software should be orchestrated.

Refer Chapter 10 to see how the tuning process is integrated as part of SDLC.

4.1.6. Multimedia Representations

All the aspects interface metaphor mentioned from 4.1.1 to 4.1.5 together determine the depiction representations through multimedia. Various types of multimedia representations are mentioned below.

> **Icon (I)**
> **Visual (V)**
> **Animation (An)**
> **Audio (A)**
> **Text (T)**
> **Hypertext (HT)**
> **Layout (L)**
> **Interface Programming (IP)**
> **Functionality (Fn)**

Icons, Visuals, Animation, Audio, Text and Hypertext are commonly used for designing the graphical user interfaces. Interface programming is essential in places where the user interface is required to visually or by any other means indicate the state of a process. It is also required in situations where the user interface dynamically changes to adjust with the user needs. Many times the interface metaphor influences entire functionality of software. The software is designed to emulate the behavior of a real life object.

Discussion

This chapter has presented the reasons of why an interface metaphor projects different images, highlights different similarities, and offers different quality of experiences [Madsen, 2000], when used in different software products. The tuning process interweaves various aspects of interface metaphor, with certain elements of software, and the requirements of specified user. Appendix C. presents a detailed comparative study of 'book' metaphor and its varied applications. Thus, we have defined the aspects and determinants of so-called illusion or magic [Marchak, 2000] [Madsen, 2000] of interface metaphor. The determinants of tuning set the coordinates for visualization of interface metaphor. **The tuning process assists the user interface designer in selecting proper viewpoint, focusing on correct affordances, adjusting the flavor and tone, and controlling the fusion of interface metaphor. It helps in deciding from where to view, what to include and exclude, what to focus and ignore and how to represent the interface metaphor using multimedia. It enables the interface designer in crafting the desired user experience.**

Chapter 5. Analysis of Interface Metaphor

5.1 Dissection of Interface Metaphor

After selecting and tuning the aspects of interface metaphor, it is taken up for detailed analysis. This chapter provides a method for concept-by-concept analysis through the dissection of interface metaphor. Following are the objectives of the dissection.

5.1.1. Objectives of Metaphor Dissection

- To find cross-domain mappings between design model[14] and user's model[15].
- To observe and regulate the tradeoffs between interface metaphor and software.
- To measure the coverage of metaphor.
- To provide objective basis for evaluation of interface metaphor.
- To achieve proper fusion between user and design models.

Donald Norman [1988] has stated the need of fusing both the design and user's models but he does not provide the process step by step. Juxtapositioning of the Commentary of Task Performance (CTP) and Interface Play Script (IPS) as shown in earlier chapter initiates this fusion. But it can be done more effectively through the dissection of interface metaphor. George Lakoff et al. [1980] introduced the term cross-domain mappings[16] in their book on linguistic metaphors. We have retained this term considering its suitability and popularity. But Lakoff et al. have not covered interface metaphors and the requirements of pre-facto analysis in software engineering context.

5.1.2. Preparation

User interface designer should have collected following inputs before starting to dissect the interface metaphor.

---

[14] The design model is the designer's conceptual model.
[15] The user's model is the mental model developed through interaction with the system [Norman, 1988].
[16] Comparison of similar concepts between the known and unknown domains.

- Selection of interface metaphors through the five steps described in earlier chapters namely-- identification of most common knowledge dimensions of users, identification of *candidate interface metaphors*, classification based on interrelationship, categorization based on animate or inanimate metaphors, assessment based on the levels of conceptual structure.

- Tuning the aspects of interface metaphor like perspective, focus, field of view and affordances (other aspects like flavor and tone are required during multimedia rendering of interface metaphor).

- Briefly defined titles of software requirements.

5.1.3. Format for Metaphor Dissection

It is necessary to create a table that has four columns namely Application Domain, Reference Domain, Metaphor Category and Multimedia Representation. In the context of interface metaphor, Application Domain and Reference Domain represent the Design Model and User's Model respectively. The first column provides the serial numbers of Cross-Domain Mappings (CDMs). Second column 'Requirement ID' mentions the serial numbers or the IDs of software requirements. These are important as the requirements analyst usually refers them by their IDs. Third column called 'Application Domain' enlists the software requirements. The forth column called 'Reference Domain' enlists the fragmented concepts of the metaphor. The fifth column called 'Metaphor Category' enlists the categories of metaphors based on the levels of conceptual structure as discussed earlier in section 3.4. The sixth column 'Multimedia Representation' is used for indicating how the particular concept of metaphor can be depicted through various media.

Initially, the dissection of concepts happens at a very superficial level in case of *Domain, Conglomerate and Multitudinous conceptual structures*. User interface designer has to select certain metaphorical concepts and dissect them further using similar format as described above.

The software requirements and concepts are juxtaposed in separate tables titled as Cross-Domain Mappings (CDMs), Unmapped Concepts (UCs), Unmapped Requirements (URs) and Dissection Termination (DT). These terms are defined in the following discussion.

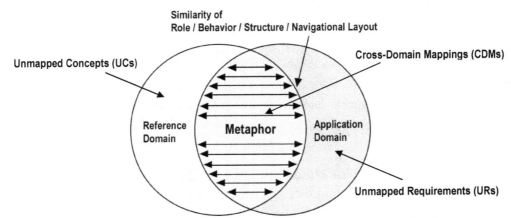

Figure 5.1 Insight into the dissection of interface metaphor

5.1.3.1. Cross-Domain Mappings (CDMs)

The user interface designer has to juxtapose each software requirement in front of the metaphorical concept where the conceptual similarities are found. All such corresponding items between application and reference domains are brought together in a separate table. These are called as Cross-Domain Mappings (CDMs).

5.1.3.2. Unmapped Concepts (UCs)

Concepts not forming meaningful correspondence with the listed software requirements remain unmapped and unutilized. The user interface designer still finds them potentially useful for future versions of software. Such unmapped concepts are arranged in a separate table. They are called as Unmapped Concepts (UCs). These concepts can be utilized during the future versions of software.

5.1.3.3. Unmapped Requirements (URs)

Software requirements not forming meaningful correspondence with the interface metaphor remain unmapped. These are called as Unmapped Requirements (URs) and arranged in a separate table. Identification of Unmapped Requirements (URs) defines the scope for exploring supporting interface metaphors to be used in combination with the present interface metaphor. In such a situation, one comes across diverse metaphors as introduced during the classification of interface metaphors in section 3.3.

5.1.3.4. Dissection Termination (DT) point

The dissection of interface metaphor is continued till the user interface designer finds relevant and apparently usable concepts. When the concepts begin to lose their relevance with software scope, the dissection activity is stopped at that point, which is referred as Dissection Termination (DT) point. Basically, (s)he has to expand the field of view of interface metaphor to match with the software scope. Dissection Termination (DT) point is also decided by the boundaries of software scope. User interface designer realizes whether the field of view of interface metaphor is adequate for the software scope or not during dissection. In case of diverse interface metaphors the Dissection Termination (DT) point is reached too early.

5.1.3.5. Terminus Concept

Endpoint of a branch within the conceptual structure is called as the terminus concept. Actually there is no such endpoint, as the conceptual structure can always be broken down further. But the terminus concept is a point where interface designer prefers to end the branch of the conceptual structure. It is also a point where interface designer deviates from the regular conceptual structure and goes beyond the constraints of the metaphor, as discussed in chapter 4.

5.1.3.6. Structural categories

The abbreviations of structural categories to be used during the dissection are given below.

Domain (D), Conglomerate (C), Multitudinous (M), Animate Singleton (AS), Inanimate Singleton (IS), Flat concept (F)

5.1.3.7. Multimedia Representations

It is necessary to indicate the type of multimedia representation in front of every Cross-Domain Mapping (CDM). This input helps in identification of creative and technical skills required for design and development of the interface metaphor. **The types of multimedia can be indicated using following abbreviations.**

Icon (I), Visual (V), Animation (An), Audio (A), Text (T), Hypertext (HT), Layout (L), Interface Programming (IP), Functionality (Fn)

5.1.4. Precautions For Metaphor Dissection

User interface designer should take following precautions while dissecting the interface metaphor.

1. Avoid long titles

At times, the titles of software requirements are very long. In such case, user interface designer should try to optimize on usage of words without any loss of information. At the same time, maintain the original document or IDs of software requirements. Software requirements may be arranged in the same order as they were found or briefed by the user.

2. Avoid duplication

At times, same software requirement appears twice with different style of wording. It should be verified minutely and then removed from the list.

3. Avoid metaphoric expressions

Incautiously, the user, analyst and user interface designer use metaphoric expressions while framing the software requirements. Such expressions should be noted separately and removed. During the formation of Cross-Domain Mappings (CDMs), such metaphoric expressions in the list of software requirements cause confusion.

For example, a software requirement was titled as shown in Figure 5.2 on its left side during the dissection of classroom metaphor.

CDM 4.	4.	Reference letter (on/off)	4. Tracing paper, Stencil

Figure 5.2 Metaphors in the wording of requirements

Here the 'stencil' is a metaphoric concept. The intension is to provide reference of an alphabet in the background like the stencil to guide the user in drawing. The requirement was reworded as shown in Figure 5.3 and the term 'stencil' was shifted under the metaphor column.

CDM 4.	4.	Stencil of letter for practice (on/off)	Tracing paper

Figure 5.3 Re-wording the requirement

4. Avoid linguistic metaphors

While forming the Cross-Domain Mappings (CDMs), user interface designer should stress more on finding conceptual similarities. It is very likely that one ends up forming linguistic metaphors as the dissection activity relies on lexical representations. The linguistic metaphors are also part of the activity but they should be documented separately as shown in Chapter 7.

5. Highlight conceptual similarities

While fragmenting the metaphoric concepts, the user interface designer should highlight the similarities using minimum words.

6. Be flexible to change

Several revisions are required for organizing the Cross-Domain Mappings (CDMs), Unmapped Concept (UCs) and Unmapped Requirements (URs). User interface designer should be flexible to modify the dissected work as new insights keep emerging.

The dissection of various types of interface metaphors is presented in the following sections of this chapter.

5.2 Dissection of Coherent Interface Metaphor

		Table 5.1 Dissection of 'Classroom' as Interface Metaphor for Inscript Typing Tutor Software [Katre, 2005] (Coherent Metaphor with *Multitudinous Conceptual Structure*.)			
		Cross Domain Mappings (CDMs)			
CDM Nos.	**Req. IDs**	**Application Domain** *Requirement Titles*	**Reference Domain** *Classroom*	**Meta. Cat.**	**MM Rep.**
CDM 1.	1.	Introduction to Indian Scripts	Book	IS	L, V
CDM 2.	2.	Demonstrate writing	Blackboard	F	L, V
CDM 3.	3.	Drawing area for practice	Slate / Notebook	F	L, V
CDM 4.	4.	Reference of letter (on/off)	Tracing paper, Stencil	F	I, V
CDM 5.	5.	Draw tool	Pencil	IS	I, Fn
CDM 6.	6.	Erase drawing	Duster	F	IP, I
CDM 7.	7.	Refresh	New clean slate	F	I
CDM 8.	8.	Typing speed	Stopwatch	F	I, V
CDM 9.	9.	Open drawing	Taking it from drawer	F	IP, An
CDM 10.	10.	Authentication of certificate	Signature of Examiner	F	V, T
CDM 11.	11.	Save current state of work	Packing the schoolbag	F	IP, An
CDM 12.	12.	Provide guidance & tips	Teacher / Typing Expert	AS	* Role
CDM 13.	13.	Register User Name	Enrolment in the class	IS	Fn, I
CDM 14.	14.	Save settings (slate, pencil, color)	Keeping it in toolbox	F	IP, An
CDM 15.	15.	Save my typing / writing	Keeping it in the drawer	F	IP, An
CDM 16.	16.	Show demo and drawing area	Blackboard & Slate	F	IP, L
CDM 17.	17.	View demo only	Teacher only (Blackboard)	F	IP, L
CDM 18.	18.	View my drawing area only	Student only (Slate)	F	IP, L
CDM 19.	19.	Build letter forms with components	Puzzle / Game /Quiz	M	-
CDM 20.	20.	Visual Key pressing by mouse	Key pressing sound	F	A
CDM 21.	21.	Warning signal	Teacher's Whistle	F	A
CDM 22.	22.	Performance evaluation	Mark sheet and Certificate	IS	L
CDM 23.	23.	Tools	Toolbox	IS	IP, L, I
CDM 24.	24.	Log maintenance	Attendance Register	IS	Fn, V, L, I

Before starting to dissect the 'classroom' metaphor, the author of this dissertation has followed the selection and tuning process as discussed earlier. The outcome is documented in Appendix D. Only after finishing these activities, the dissection of 'classroom' metaphor is carried out.

In Table 5.1, the software requirements are arranged under the column of 'Application Domain' in the same order as they were discovered. Metaphoric concepts within the 'classroom' metaphor are placed in front of the requirements where they seem to resonate conceptually. All the metaphoric concepts are coherent as they are interrelated.

Signs like – and ? are used in places where there is lack of clarity. *Conglomerate, Multitudinous and Singleton Conceptual Structures* need to be dissected in further levels. CDM 12 shown in Table 5.1 is actually an *Animate Metaphor*.

		Table 5.2 Unmapped Requirements (URs) of 'Classroom' Metaphor	
UR Nos.	**Req. IDs**	**Application Domain** *Requirement Titles*	**Reference Domain** *Classroom*
UR 1.	25.	Undo / Redo writing	
UR 2.	26.	Reduce / Increase drawing speed	
UR 3.	27.	Next and previous letter animation	
UR 4.	28.	Indicate vowels, consonants, *Matras*	**No Matching Concepts**
UR 5.	29.	Display keyboard map	
UR 6.	30.	Writing practice	
UR 7.	31.	Print my name	
UR 8.	32.	Mute sounds	

It is marked differently to indicate that it needs to be dissected separately. The requirement IDs mentioned in Table 5.1 and Table 5.2 are kept sequential for the convenience of counting in the context of the dissertation. Usually the sequence of requirement IDs gets disturbed during the dissection activity.

Table 5.2 shows the list of Unmapped Requirements (URs). But all these may not always remain Unmapped Requirements (URs). As one progresses further in the process of visualization, new mapping possibilities are realized. The total number of Unmapped Requirements (URs) is likely to reduce.

Table 5.3 shows the Unmapped Concepts (UCs) of 'classroom' and related metaphors surfaced during the dissection activity. The dissection activity is terminated at UC 16., as thereafter the concepts appeared irrelevant and too much beyond the software scope. The Dissection Termination (DT) point outlines the boundary of the **field of view** of classroom metaphor.

Table 5.3 Unmapped Concepts (UCs) of 'Classroom' Metaphor				
Application Domain *Requirement Titles*	**UC Nos.**	**Reference Domain** *Classroom*	**Meta. Cat.**	**MM Rep.**
	UC 1.	Scale	F	IP, V
	UC 2.	Library	M	-
	UC 3.	Notice Board	IS	IP, L, I
	UC 4.	Graffiti	IS	IP, L
	UC 5.	Homework	IS	?
	UC 6.	Other students	?	-
	UC 7.	Examiner	AS	-
No Matching Requirements	**UC 8.**	Bell	F	A, V
⟵	**UC 9.**	Attendance Register	IS	L
	UC 10.	Assembly Hall	M	-
	UC 11.	Schedule / Calendar	IS	L, IP
	UC 12.	Charts	IS	V
	UC 13.	Clock	F	V, IP, An
	UC 14.	Staff room	M	-
	UC 15.	Craft Material	IS	V
	UC 16.	Computer Lab	M	-
		(DT) ↓		

Table 5.4 and Table 5.5 show how the second level dissection is carried out for CDM 1 and CDM 5, which are 'Book' and 'Pencil' respectively. During this process new software requirements were found out (Req. ID 33 to 39).

Table 5.4 Second Level Dissection of CDM 1

CDM Nos.	Req. IDs	Application Domain *Requirement Titles*	Reference Domain *Book*	Meta. Cat.	MM Rep.
CDM 1.1	33.	Index	Index	F	HT
CDM 1.2	34.	Text	Multiple Pages	F	L
CDM 1.3	35.	Next and Previous	Page Turning	F	IP, I, L
CDM 1.4	36.	Print	Get me a copy	F	Fn, I
No Matching Requirements			Bookmark	F	IP, L
			Annotations	F	T, IP, L
			Book Cover	F	L
			(DT)		

Table 5.5 Second Level Dissection of CDM 5

CDM Nos.	Req. IDs	Application Domain *Requirement Titles*	Reference Domain *Pencil*	Meta. Cat.	MM Rep.
CDM 5.1	37.	Change ink color	Different ink bottles	F	Fn, I
CDM 5.2	38.	Drawing / Writing	Screeching sound of pencil	F	Fn, I, A
CDM 5.3	39.	Define stroke type	Cut nibs (Calligraphic strokes)	F	Fn, I
No Matching Requirements			Change the tip size	F	Fn, I
			(DT)		

At this point the dissection of coherent interface metaphor is completed. User interface designer can go on dissecting the conceptual structure of the interface metaphor in further levels if it is necessary. In the next section of this chapter, we have shown the dissection of diverse interface metaphors.

5.3   Dissection of Animate Metaphor

So far we have discussed the behavioral attributes of *Inanimate Metaphors*. In several projects, the software has to replace a human role, which is an integral part of a business process. The software has to perform similar role or activities as a human being. But many projects ignore the human roles and end up computerizing only the business processes. **We call such human roles as *Animate Metaphors*. Dissection of such interface metaphor can be extremely helpful during requirements elaboration and conceptualizing the behavior of software.**

For example, during the dissection of 'classroom' metaphor in Table 5.1, we have marked 'teacher' (CDM 12) as *Animate Metaphor*. The tutoring software will be incomplete without the 'teacher' like behavior. Therefore, the traits of a teacher are dissected and mapped with the existing software requirements. It shows the possibility of extending the functionality of software further to emulate the behavioral qualities of 'teacher' for enhancing the usability of software [Katre, 2005]

The format for dissection of *Animate Metaphor* has three columns namely CDM Nos., Traits, Actions and Requirement Titles as shown in Table 5.6. Traits and actions are the new terms that we associate with *Animate Metaphor*. These are defined below.

5.3.1.   Traits
Traits are the distinguishable characteristics of an individual assigned with a specific responsibility. For example, a salesman has to be business minded, negotiating, convincing and polite. Some of the traits of a teacher are identified as to teach, observe, administer, guide, encourage, inspire, entertain and evaluate. These traits are universally accepted and they are found in all good teachers. One should not mingle the traits of an individual with the traits of the role that (s)he plays.

5.3.2.   Actions
Each trait can be fragmented in terms of certain key actions and sub-actions. Metaphorical incorporation of these actions in software can help capturing the particular trait.

Dissecting the *Animate Metaphor* is quite different than the dissection of coherent and diverse interface metaphors. But the aspects of tuning of interface metaphor are applicable without any change.

Table 5.6 Dissection of *Animate Metaphor* (CDM 12)		
Traits	**Reference Domain** *Teacher (Actions)* ⟵	⟶ **Application Domain** *Requirement Titles*
1. Teach	**1.1 Knowledge sharing and demonstration** ▪ **Brief intro. to Indian Scripts** ▪ **How to draw the letters** ▪ **Typing guidelines**	▪ **Brief intro. to Indian Scripts** ▪ **Show how to draw letters** ▪ **Provide basic guidelines**
	1.2 Ask surprise questions	
	1.3 Quote examples	**No Connecting Behavior**
	1.4 Give assignments	▪ **Practice / Assignments**
2. Observe	**2.1 Point out the aspects not explored** ▪ **The keys not practiced** ▪ **Lessons not studied** ▪ **Lessons not practiced** ▪ **Practice without looking at the keyboard**	Highlight - ▪ **The keys not practiced** ▪ **Lessons not studied** ▪ **Lessons not practiced**
	2.2 Point out mistakes in- ▪ **Typing** ▪ **Use of fingers** ▪ **Sitting posture**	▪ **Identify the typing errors**
	2.3 Point out the weakness of a student (knowledge of language, skills, concentration)	**No Connecting Behavior**
3. Administer	**3.1 Maintain the attendance register**	▪ **Maintain log of usage by the learner**
	3.2 Check regularity of students	▪ **Use log data for checking the regularity**
	3.3 Punish irregular student	**No Connecting Behavior**
4. Guide	**4.1 Give simple tips on typing**	▪ **Tips on typing**
	4.2 Find the difficulty of students	
	4.3 Suggest improvements	**No Connecting Behavior**
5. Encourage	**5.1 Boost the moral of students**	
6. Inspire	**6.1 Demonstrate the best practices**	**No Connecting Behavior**
7. Entertain	**7.1 Introduce games**	▪ **Games and puzzles**
	7.2 Organize competitions	
	7.3 Share anecdotes / funny experiences	**No Connecting Behavior**
8. Evaluate	**8.1 Conduct tests to check speed and correctness of typing**	▪ **Evaluate the speed and correctness of typing**
	8.2 Evaluate the performance of student	▪ **Evaluate the performance through a series of tests**
	8.3 Produce a mark sheet	▪ **Produce a mark sheet**
	8.4 Offer certificate	**No Connecting Behavior**

At this point, the dissection of *animate singleton metaphor* is completed.

5.4   *Dissection of Diverse Interface Metaphors*

At times, there are several *candidate interface metaphors* but they are very diverse based on their interrelationships. Various alternatives as competing *candidate interface metaphors*; to cover the software requirements should be analyzed first. If among competing candidates none satisfies to become 'the' interface metaphor then we need to consider integration of diverse interface metaphors.

5.4.1.   Integration of Diverse Interface Metaphors

There are two types of integrating the diverse interface metaphors, which are named as **cooperative** and **incoherent** integration.

5.4.1.1.   Cooperative Integration

If the diverse interface metaphors are designed with a core interface metaphor at the center and supporting interface metaphors around it then this can be called as a cooperative integration. QuickMM Album Author dissected in this section, is an example of cooperative integration of diverse interface metaphors.

5.4.1.2.   Incoherent Integration

If the diverse interface metaphors are integrated without any logical connection or the design of core and supporting interface metaphors then it can be called as incoherent integration. Applications designed with random approach are likely to emerge as examples of incoherent integration of diverse interface metaphors. This type of integration can be useful in designing interesting applications for children.

5.4.2.   Cooperative Integration of Diverse Interface Metaphors

5.4.2.1.   Core Interface Metaphor

Among all candidate interface metaphors, the one, which precisely focuses on the main functionalities of software, is called as core interface metaphor. It captures the central theme of software. It gives proper thematic orientation to software developer, interface designer and users. Diverse metaphors without the core interface metaphor produce a disoriented product. For example, QuickMM Album Author [Katre, 2001] software maintains 'album' as its core metaphor.

5.4.2.2.   Supporting Interface Metaphors

The candidate interface metaphors, which contribute new affordances and enrich the conceptual structure of core metaphor, are referred as supporting interface metaphors. Usually, in case of diverse metaphors, the core metaphor is inadequate to map all software requirements. In order to map the Unmapped Requirements (URs), user interface designer has to consider other interface metaphors that reinforce the core metaphor and add interesting dimensions to it without disturbing its focus. The core metaphor borrows new concepts and affordances from the supporting interface metaphors. For example, exhibition, greeting card and calendar serve as supporting interface metaphors in case of QuickMM Album Author software. They provide super-affordances to 'Album' as the core interface metaphor as explained in Chapter 4.

5.4.2.3.   Conceptual Proximity and Alignment

Conceptual proximity means, conceptual closeness between the core and supporting metaphors. They should not be completely disjointed or conveying contrary concepts. Conceptual alignment means, establishing a metaphorical relation or orienting in line with the core interface metaphor. The supporting interface metaphors need to be conceptually aligned with the core interface metaphor. It helps in the fusion affordances between the both kinds of interface metaphors.

QuickMM Album Author software exemplifies the use of diverse interface metaphors. It combines Album, Exhibition, Greeting Card and Calendar metaphors together. The activity started with 'Album' metaphor only but new metaphors were conceived due to large number of Unmapped Requirements (URs). Details of selection and tuning of metaphors for QuickMM Album Author are given in Appendix D2.

The author of this dissertation has dissected 'Album' as core interface metaphor and 'exhibition, greeting card and calendar' as supporting metaphors in the Tables 5.6, 5.7, 5.8, 5.9 and 5.10.

Table 5.7 Dissection of Album Metaphor (*Inanimate Singleton*)

Core Interface Metaphor
Cross Domain Mappings (CDMs)

CDM Nos.	Req. IDs	Application Domain *Requirement Titles*	Reference Domain *Album*	Meta. Cat.	MM Rep.
CDM 1.	1.	Image for start / end of presentation	Front and back album cover	F	V
CDM 2.	2.	Collection of templates with layouts	Pockets for photo insertion	F	Fn
CDM 3.	3.	Categorization of content	Themes, Events	F	V, Fn
CDM 4.	4.	Mouse-over / hotspots	Recognize the persons	F	Fn
CDM 5.	5.	Theme based backgrounds and cursors	Album styles	F	V, Fn, L
CDM 6.	6.	Encryption of all the contents	Lamination of photos	F	Fn
CDM 7.	7.	Making an executable	Binding the album	F	Fn
CDM 8.	8.	Store Favorites	Bookmark	F	V, Fn
CDM 9.	9.	Hierarchical structure	Family tree, Event schedule	S	Fn
CDM 10.	10.	Captions, Narration	Storyline	F	T

Table 5.8 Dissection of Exhibition Metaphor (*Multitudinous*)

Supporting Interface Metaphor
Cross Domain Mappings (CDMs)

CDM Nos.	Req. IDs	Application Domain *Requirement Titles*	Reference Domain *Exhibition*	Meta. Cat.	MM Rep.
CDM 11.	11.	Integration of collections	Collections of albums	F	Fn, I, L
CDM 12.	12.	Comments, Annotations	Visitor's book	F	Fn, T
CDM 13.	13.	Presenting selected images and video clips	Gallery	F	Fn, I
CDM 14.	14.	Auto-play in loop	Walk through the exhibits	F	Fn
CDM 15.	15.	Publish a website	Exhibit for all	F	Fn

No Matching Requirements ⟵   ↓ (DT)

Table 5.9 Dissection of Greeting Card Metaphor (*Inanimate Singleton*)

		Supporting Interface Metaphor Cross Domain Mappings (CDMs)			
CDM Nos.	Req. IDs	**Application Domain** *Requirement Titles*	**Reference Domain** *Greeting Card*	Meta. Cat.	MM Rep.
CDM 16.	16.	Layout options, Styles	Card themes	F	Fn, V, L, I
CDM 17.	17.	Messages	Greetings	F	T, V
CDM 18.	18.	e-mail	Post it	F	Fn, I

Table 5.10 Dissection of Calendar Metaphor (*Inanimate Singleton*)

		Supporting Interface Metaphor Cross Domain Mappings (CDMs)			
CDM Nos.	Req. IDs	**Application Domain** *Requirement Titles*	**Reference Domain** *Calendar*	Meta. Cat.	MM Rep.
CDM 19.	19.	Change photos daily, weekly, monthly from desktop	Pages of a calendar	F	Fn, V, L
CDM 20.	20.	Location on the desktop	Display it on wall or on table	F	Fn, V, L
CDM 21.	21.	Remind important dates and send messages	Send birthday greeting cards	F	Fn

Table 5.11 Unmapped Requirements (URs) of QuickMM Album Author

UR Nos.	Req. IDs	**Application Domain** *Requirement Titles*	**Reference Domains** *(Album, Exhibition, Greeting Card, Calendar)*
UR 1.	22.	Print Screen	
UR 2.	23.	Save Image / Clip on Disk	
UR 3.	24.	View only / presentation mode	
UR 4.	25.	Editable file for author	**No Matching Concepts**
UR 5.	26.	Capture the fonts used for captions	
UR 6.	27.	Create a screensaver using any picture from the album	
UR 7.	28.	Create a wallpaper for desktop	
UR 8.	29.	Select the image	

We have completed the dissection of diverse interface metaphor at this point. An example of dissecting the *Animate Metaphor* is given in the next section.

Discussion

The dissection classroom interface metaphor reveals the levels within the *multitudinous conceptual structure.* **It also reveals the cognitive map of 'classroom' from the viewpoint of the school children in India. The importance of tuning the aspects of interface metaphor like focus, perspective, and field of view is conveyed through this example.** One can witness the matching of boundaries between the **software scope** and **field of view** of metaphor at the end of Cross-Domain Mappings (CDMs). **The Terminus concept of every Cross-Domain Mapping (CDM) and Dissection Termination (DT) point establishes that the Unmapped Concepts (UCs) are beyond the existing software scope and field of view of interface metaphor.** The list of Unmapped Concepts (UCs) already includes some concepts like library, staff room, and computer lab that are beyond the field of view. The terminology of CDMs, UCs, URs, Terminus and DT Point give proper insight into the dissection activity.

The second level dissection included examples of both **inanimate** and **animate metaphors.** Dissection of *Animate Metaphor* like 'teacher' shows how the behavior of human role can be fragmented in terms of **traits** and **actions** for conceptualizing the behavior of software.

Dissection of QuickMM Album Author showed how the supporting interface metaphors like exhibition, calendar, and greeting card have added super-affordances to album as core interface metaphor. This is an example of cooperative integration of diverse interface metaphors. Metaphoric concepts like e-mailing a selected photograph from the 'multimedia album' as a digital greeting card; publishing a website of multimedia albums as an 'exhibition'; creating a 'calendar' using selected photographs for display on the desktop; show how the supporting interface metaphors can enrich the conceptual structure of the album interface metaphor.

The examples presented in this chapter also prove the classes of interface metaphors namely *coherent* and *diverse* are based on cognitive maps.

Chapter 6. Quantitative Evaluation of Interface Metaphor

Concept-by-concept dissection of interface metaphor provides objective basis for its quantitative evaluation contrary to intuitive approach of interface designers. Researchers like Marcus [1994, 1995, 1998, 2002], Vaantinen [1994], Madsen [1994], Smilowitz [1996] and many others have emphatically stated the lack of theoretical basis for the evaluation of interface metaphors. **Therefore, a technique for quantification of interface metaphor is evolved. It is based on the outcome of the concept by concept dissection of interface metaphor as performed in the previous chapter. One can derive several inferences with regard to the potential, coverage, applicability and extensibility of interface metaphor based on the quantitative evaluation.**

6.1 Elements of Quantification

Dissection of interface metaphor is a prerequisite activity before the quantitative evaluation. (S)he has to quantify the dissected outcome as given below.

Dissection of interface metaphor (first level):

Count the total number of-

1. Software Requirements (presented under 'application domain')
2. Metaphoric Concepts (presented under 'reference domain')
3. Cross-Domain Mappings (CDMs)
4. Unmapped Concepts (UCs)
5. Unmapped Requirements (URs)

Dissection of individual CDMs:

Count the total number of-

1. Cross-Domain Mappings (CDMs) taken up for second level dissection
2. New Software Requirements identified (presented under 'application domain')

3. New Metaphoric Concepts identified (presented under 'reference domain')

4. Cross-Domain Mappings (CDMs)

5. Unmapped Concepts (UCs)

6. Unmapped Requirements (URs)

Quantifying the types of multimedia representations:

Multimedia representations proposed in front of every CDM may be counted based on each type.

Quantification of categories based on the levels of conceptual structures:

Count the levels of Conceptual Structures -

1. *Domain*

2. *Conglomerate*

3. *Multitudinous*

4. *Inanimate Singleton*

5. *Animate Singleton*

6. *Flat Concepts*

A separate table may be prepared to present the aggregate figures. In the following sections of this chapter, quantitative evaluations of coherent/*multitudinous conceptual structure*, diverse/*inanimate singleton conceptual structures* and *animate singleton conceptual structure* dissected in Chapter 5. are presented.

We are introducing a few more new terms such as Conceptual Bandwidth, Usable Conceptual bandwidth, Coverage of Interface Metaphor in the context of quantitative evaluation. These are explained in the following points.

6.1.1.   Conceptual Bandwidth

The total number of concepts emerged out of the dissection of interface metaphor are called as its conceptual bandwidth. It is relevant only in the context of the software project for which the interface metaphor is dissected. The same interface metaphor can provide different amount of conceptual bandwidth depending on the perspective, focus and field of view that vary from project to project, as explained in chapter 4.

6.1.2. Usable Conceptual Bandwidth

The total number of Cross-Domain Mappings (CDMs) formed during the dissection activity defines the usable conceptual bandwidth of interface metaphor.

6.1.3. Coverage of Interface Metaphor

This is the total percentage of software requirements mapped with the interface metaphor gives you the coverage of interface metaphor.

6.1.3.1. Rating the Coverage of Interface Metaphor

Ratings can be given on the basis of the percentage of coverage offered by the interface metaphor. The guidelines for rating the coverage of interface metaphor are given below.

Table 6.1 Rating the coverage	
0% to 20%	Poor
20% to 40%	Average
40% to 60%	Good
60% to 80%	Excellent
80% to 100%	Outstanding

If the coverage is less than 40% then users are likely to fail in comprehending the overall interface metaphor. During our testing, the subjects require continuous exposure of minimum 30 to 40% of the concepts to be able to guess the complete metaphor[17]. Minimum 30% to 40% of exposure of the conceptual structure is sufficient to activate the right cognitive map for the average users. The metaphoric concepts get scattered between the Unmapped Requirements (URs) and become unnoticeable. Users fail to correlate the scattered metaphoric concepts. It fails to invoke the cognitive map in the minds of users.

---

[17] We required mentioning of minimum concepts like desk, schoolbag and blackboard for the subjects to be able to guess that the classroom is being described.

User interface designer has to ensure that the coverage of interface metaphor is at least in the range of 40% to 60% (Good) while selecting it. If it is rated as *average* or *poor* then the user interface designer should consider different alternatives or go for diverse metaphors, e.g., 'album' metaphor used in QuickMM Album Author (Katre, 2001) barely covers 34% of requirements (see 6.4.2).

The 'classroom' metaphor is offering a total coverage of 80% (Refer 6.2.1). Therefore it is rated as an *outstanding* interface metaphor for Inscript Typing Tutor software.

6.2 *Quantitative Evaluation of Coherent Interface Metaphor*

Elements mentioned in Section 6.1 are quantified for the 'classroom' interface metaphor dissected in Section 5.2, Chapter 5.

6.2.1. Quantitative Evaluation of 'Classroom' Metaphor

Table 6.2 Quantification of First Level Dissection (Refer Tables 5.1, 5.2, 5.3)			
Application Domain	**Total**	**Reference Domain**	**Total**
Soft. Requirements	32	Metaphoric Concepts	$40 + n$
Mapped Soft. Requirements	24	Mapped Metaphoric Concepts	24
Total No. of URs	8	Total No. of UCs	$16 + n$

Table 6.3 Quantification of Second Level Dissection (CDM1+5) (Refer Table 5.4 and Table 5.5)			
Application Domain	**Total**	**Reference Domain**	**Total**
No. of CDMs selected for second level dissection			2
New Soft. Requirements	7	New Metaphoric Concepts	11
Mapped Soft. Requirements	7	Mapped Metaphoric Concepts	7
Total No. of URs	0	Total No. of UCs	4

Total count of Tables 6.2 and 6.3 is presented in Table 6.4.

Table 6.4 Aggregate Projections			
Application Domain	**Total**	**Reference Domain**	**Total**
Soft. Requirements	39	Metaphoric Concepts	51
Mapped Soft. Requirements	31	Mapped Metaphoric Concepts	31
Total No. of URs	8	Total No. of UCs	20

Total conceptual bandwidth of 'classroom' metaphor = 51 Concepts

Total usable conceptual bandwidth of 'classroom' metaphor = 31 CDMs

Coverage of 'classroom' metaphor = 80%

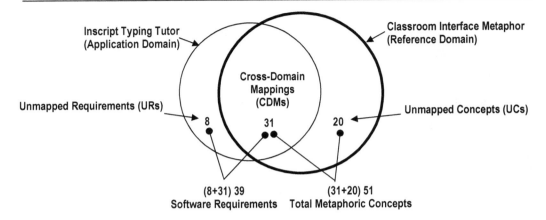

Figure 6.1 Aggregate projections of 'classroom' interface metaphor

It is possible to draw a variety of inferences and develop new insights through the quantitative evaluation of 'classroom' interface metaphor. We have also dissected and quantified several other interface metaphors to arrive at the inferences given below. These are true for all coherent interface metaphors.

6.2.2.   Proportion of A and B

Declaration:
- **A stands for Metaphoric Concepts**
- **B stands for Software Requirements**

(Coherent Metaphor Case)

If A > B then

1. The coherent interface metaphor has adequate potential and it can provide good coverage for the given software.

2. There is bound to be some Unmapped Concepts (UCs) that can be utilized for future versions of software. The interface metaphor is extendible.

(Diverse Metaphor Case)

If A < B then

3. The metaphor may not have adequate potential for the given software.

4. One might require using diverse interface metaphors.

6.2.3. Proportion of Coverage Versus Usage

Percentages of coverage of the metaphor and usage of metaphoric concepts can be projected as shown in Figure 6.2. and Figure 6.3.

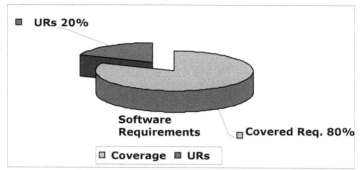

Figure 6.2 Proportion of Software Requirements covered by metaphor

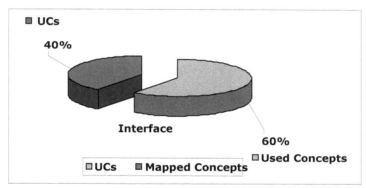

Figure 6.3 Proportion of Usage of metaphoric concepts

Declaration:

- **C stands for percentage of covered software requirements**
- **D stands for percentage of used metaphoric concepts**

Following inferences can be drawn.

If C > D then

1. The metaphor is well synchronized with the proposed software.

If C < D then

2. Scope for enhancements in the interface metaphor possible. Supporting metaphors may be needed.

6.2.4.   Proportions of Structural Categories

Table 6.5 Proportion of Structural Categories (Refer Tables 5.1, 5.4, 5.5)	
Domain (D)	None
Conglomerate (C)	None
Multitudinous (M)	6
Inanimate Singleton (IS)	13
Animate Singleton (AS)	2
Flat (F)	30

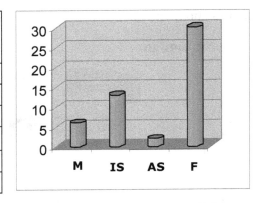

Chart 6.4 Proportions of metaphor categories

Usually the *Multitudinous* and Animate *Singleton Conceptual Structures* are very less in number if compared with *Inanimate Singleton Conceptual Structure and Flat Concepts*. *Flat Concepts* are always the largest in number. This trend is common in most interface metaphors.

6.2.5.   Quantifying the Types of Multimedia Representation

Counting the types of multimedia representation is helpful in visualizing technical and creative skills required for developing the interface. For example, some Cross-Domain Mappings (CDMs) demand special interface programming effort. Some Cross-Domain Mappings (CDMs) amount to developing entire functionality itself. These can complicate the software design issues. Quantifying the types of multimedia representation helps the project manager in anticipating the provision of resources like time, manpower and finance. Table 6.6 shows the occurrence of various types of multimedia representations in the 'classroom' metaphor.

Table 6.6 Counting the Types of Multimedia Representation (Refer Tables 5.1, 5.4, 5.5)	
Icon (I)	15
Visual (V)	12
Animation (An)	5
Audio (A)	4
Text (T)	2
Hyper Text (HT)	1
Layout (L)	18
Interface Programming (IP)	17
Functionality (F)	8

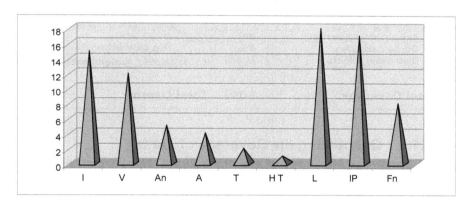

Figure 6.5 Proposed types of multimedia representation

Figure 6.5 provides a graphical representation of Table 6.6.

At this point, we have finished the quantitative evaluation of 'classroom' interface metaphor. This example also reveals the characteristics of a typical coherent metaphor with *Multitudinous Conceptual Structure*.

6.3   Quantitative Evaluation of Animate Metaphor

The 'teacher' *(Animate Metaphor)* dissected in section 5.3, Table 5.6 is quantified in terms of the coverage and depth of every trait represented in the software. This type of evaluation is slightly different than the way it is done for coherent and diverse interface metaphors. Designing the Teacher Like Behavior of e-Learning System: A Case Study of Indian Scripts Typing Tutor [Katre, 2005] elaborates how this method is helpful shaping the behavior of the system.

Table 6.7 Calculation of *Coverage* and *Depth* of Traits in Application Software (Refer Table 5.6)				
1. Teach	**1.1 Knowledge sharing and demonstration** ■ **Brief intro. to Indian Scripts** ■ **How to draw the letters** ■ **Typing guidelines**	**100%**	■ **Brief intro. to Indian Scripts** ■ **Show how to draw letters** ■ **Provide basic guidelines**	**100%**
	1.2 Ask surprise questions	0%	**No Connecting Behavior**	0%
	1.3 Quote examples	0%		
	1.4 Give assignments	100%	■ **Practice / Assignments**	**100%**
	Total Coverage	**50%**	**Total Depth**	**50%**

6.3.1.   Quantifying the Coverage of Traits

Every trait translates into a set of specific actions. The percentage of actions matching with corresponding software requirements indicates the coverage of a particular trait in the software. For example, in Table 6.7 check the trait no. 1 titled as 'teach'. It is fragmented into four actions 1.1 to 1.4. Out of these actions, 1.2 and 1.3 do not have matching software requirements. Therefore the coverage of this particular trait in the software is about 50%.

6.3.2.   Quantifying the Depth of Traits

As shown in Table 6.7, every action is fragmented further into sub-actions. Similarly the software requirements are also fragmented into sub-requirements. User interface designer should evaluate the percentage of sub-actions vis-à-vis the sub-requirements. It indicates the depth of a particular action in the software. All actions put together provide you the percentage of the trait, e.g., the 'teach' trait has only 50% depth in the proposed software.

Table 6.8 Coverage and depth of a trait in the software		
Traits	**Coverage**	**Depth**
1. Teach	50%	50%
2. Observe	66%	36%
3. Administer	66%	66%
4. Guide	33%	33%
5. Encourage	0%	0%
6. Inspire	0%	0%
7. Entertain	33%	33%
8. Evaluate	75%	75%
Averages	40%	36%
Total Behavioral Metaphor	38%	

Table 6.8 and Figure 6.6 indicate how much the software behavior is conceptualized as per the *animate singleton metaphor*. Software and interface designers can visualize new features and functionalities required for improving the coverage and depth of each trait in the software. **Percentages of both the coverage and depth of every trait can be increased by improving the user interface and functionality of the software in its subsequent versions.**

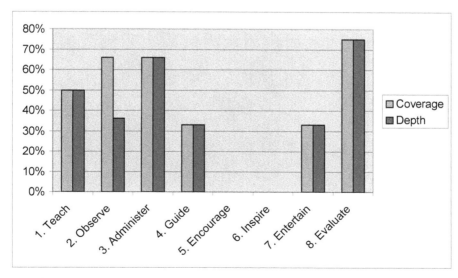

Figure 6.6 Trait wise coverage and depth of *animate metaphor*

Following inferences can be drawn based on the quantitative evaluation of 'teacher' as an *Animate Metaphor.* **The stronger, weaker and missed out traits in the software can be identified.**

Inscript Typing Tutor has fairly addressed the following traits.

- Teach
- Administer
- Evaluate

Following traits are very weak in the software.

- Observe
- Guide
- Entertain

The software does not address following traits.

- Encourage
- Inspire

At this point, we have completed the quantitative evaluation of *Animate Metaphor.*

6.4 Quantitative Evaluation of Diverse Metaphors

6.4.1. Quantitative Evaluation for QuickMM Album Author

Table 6.9 presents the aggregate projections of diverse interface metaphors dissected in Section 5.4, Chapter 5.

Table 6.9 Aggregate Projections of Diverse Metaphor			
(Refer Tables 5.7, 5.8, 5.9, 5.10, 5.11)			
Application Domain	**Total**	**Reference Domain**	**Total**
Total Software Requirements	29	Core metaphor (Table 5.6)	10
		Supporting Metaphor (Table 5.7)	5
		Supporting Metaphor (Table 5.8)	3
		Supporting Metaphor (Table 5.9)	3
		Total Metaphoric Concepts	21
Mapped Software Requirements	21	Mapped Metaphoric Concepts	21
URs	8	UCs	0

In case of diverse interface metaphors, the total of core and supporting interface metaphors has to be presented as the total number of metaphoric concepts.

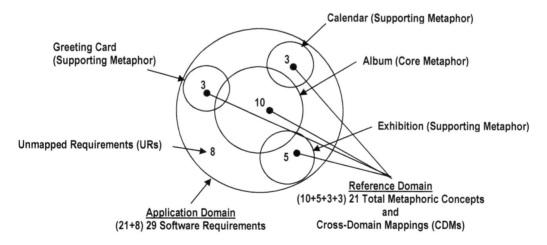

Figure 6.7 Aggregate projections of diverse metaphors

Figure 6.7 shows that the design of application and reference domains is very complex.

Total conceptual bandwidth of diverse metaphors = 21 concepts

Total usable conceptual bandwidth of diverse metaphors = 21 CDMs

Total coverage of diverse metaphors = 72%

All diverse interface metaphors together can be rated as *excellent* for QuickMM Album Author software as per the guidelines given in 6.1.3.

Following inferences can be drawn on the basis of quantitative evaluation of diverse interface metaphors. These are true for all diverse interface metaphors.

6.4.2.   Proportions of Core and Supporting Metaphors

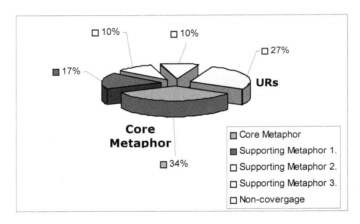

Figure 6.8 Proportion of core and supporting metaphors

Figure 6.8 shows the proportions of core metaphor, supporting metaphors and Unmapped Requirements (URs). 'Album' is the core metaphor as it contributes the largest percentage (34%) of metaphoric concepts if compared with the supporting metaphors. **It reveals a very important rule that the supporting metaphors should be downplayed than the core metaphor.** 'Exhibition' metaphor has a *Conglomerate Conceptual Structure,* which is richer than the 'album' metaphor as it provides *Singleton Conceptual Structure.* But the 'Exhibition' metaphor has been downplayed (treated as a *Flat Concept*) for not changing the scope of software.

Table 6.10 Proportion of Metaphoric Coverage Versus Usage			
Coverage	72%	Usage	100%
Unmapped Requirements (URs)	28%	Unmapped Concepts (UCs)	0%

In case of diverse interface metaphors, there are no Unmapped Concepts (UCs) left. At the same time, 28% of requirements remain unmapped. In such case, it is going to be challenging to extend the metaphoric concepts for future versions of the product. With every new requirement added, new metaphors will have to be explored.

Table 6.11 Proportion of Structural Categories (Refer Tables 5.7, 5.8, 5.9, 5.10, 5.11)	
Domain (D)	None
Conglomerate (C)	None
Multitudinous (M)	1
Inanimate Singleton (IS)	4
Animate Singleton (AS)	None
Flat concepts (F)	16

Table 6.11 corroborates with the observations given in 6.2.4. The proportion of *Multitudinous, Inanimate Singleton Conceptual Structures* and *Flat Concepts* follow similar trend in both coherent and diverse interface metaphors.

At this point, the quantitative evaluation of diverse interface metaphors chosen for QuickMM Album Author software is completed. This example has captured all the characteristics of the *cooperative integration* of diverse interface metaphors.

6.5   Trade-offs

Yousef [2001] has mentioned that a method is necessary for observing the trade-offs between the design of software and the interface metaphor so that they can be monitored. **Our systematic method of dissection, analysis and quantitative evaluation of interface metaphor proposed in this dissertation is extremely helpful in spotting the possible trade-offs.**

The said trade-offs between the software and the interface metaphor can happen in terms of re-sequencing, restructuring and identification of new software requirements. The trade-offs that happened during the dissection of 'classroom' interface metaphor are discussed in this section.

6.5.1.   Re-sequencing

Usually the software requirements get documented in the same sequence, as they are being told by the user or found by the analyst. It is a spontaneous activity. The list of requirements may not follow any logical sequence. During the software design stage, the software designer reorganizes the software requirements according to the design.

The interface metaphor can influence the sequence of requirements as per its own conceptual structure. For example, the software requirements enlisted in Table 5.1 can be re-sequenced as per the conceptual structure of 'classroom' metaphor. IDs of software requirements are mentioned for indicating the revised sequence as shown below (refer Table 6.12).

Req. IDs. 13, 24, 1, 12, 2, 3, 16, 17, 18, 23, 4, 5, 6, 7, 20, 8, 21, 14, 15, 11, 9, 22, 10

The re-sequencing has been done as per the linear order of activities related to the classroom. For example, one has to enroll in the class first, therefore 'Req. ID. 13-Register User Name' becomes the first requirement. The attendance register (Req. ID 24-Log Maintenance) comes next. It is followed by 'Req. ID 1-Introduction To Indian Scripts'. Other Req. IDs are arranged using the similar sequencing.

Table 6.12 Re-sequencing of software requirements (as per the conceptual structure of 'Classroom' Metaphor)			
Cross Domain Mappings (CDMs)			
CDM Nos.	Req. IDs	Application Domain *Requirement Titles*	Reference Domain *Classroom*
CDM 13.	13.	Register User Name	Enrolment in the class
CDM 24.	24.	Log maintenance	Attendance Register
CDM 1.	1.	Introduction to Indian Scripts	Book
CDM 12.	12.	Provide guidance & tips	Teacher / Typing Expert
CDM 2.	2.	Demonstrate writing	Blackboard
CDM 3.	3.	Drawing area for practice	Slate / Notebook
CDM 16.	16.	Show demo and drawing area	Blackboard & Slate
CDM 17.	17.	View demo only	Teacher only (Blackboard)
CDM 18	18.	View my drawing area only	Student only (Slate)
CDM 23	23.	Tools	Toolbox
CDM 4.	4.	Reference of letter (on/off)	Tracing paper, Stencil
CDM 5.	5.	Draw tool	Pencil
CDM 6.	6.	Erase drawing	Duster
CDM 7.	7.	Refresh	New clean slate
CDM 20.	20.	Visual Key pressing by mouse	Key pressing sound
CDM 8.	8.	Typing speed	Stopwatch
CDM 21	21.	Warning signal	Teacher's Whistle
CDM 14.	14.	Save settings (slate, pencil, color)	Keeping it in toolbox
CDM 15.	15.	Save my typing / writing	Keeping it in the drawer
CDM 11.	11.	Save current state of work	Packing the schoolbag
CDM 9.	9.	Open drawing	Taking it from drawer
CDM 19.	19.	Build letter forms with components	Puzzle / Game /Quiz
CDM 22.	22.	Performance evaluation	Mark sheet and Certificate
CDM 10.	10.	Authentication of certificate	Signature of Examiner

6.5.2. Restructuring

The conceptual structure of the interface metaphor can also help in restructuring the software requirements. Change in the sequence and structure of software requirements can influence the design of software. The software and user interface designers have to arrive at some compromises to address the needs of software and interface design both. Figure 6.9 shows how the classroom metaphor has restructured the software requirements of Inscript Typing Tutor.

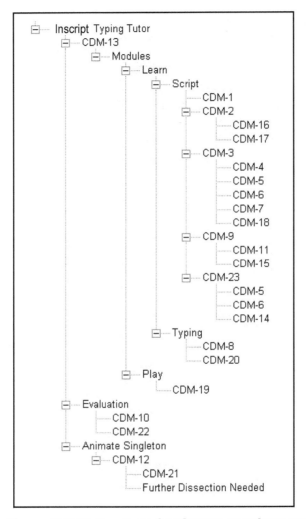

Figure 6.9 Restructured software requirements

6.5.3. Insight of New Requirements

The dissection of interface metaphor also provides insight into new software requirements. Especially, during the second and third level dissection of CDMs, the metaphor reveals concepts that indicate finer details of a particular software requirement e.g. refer Tables 5.4 and 5.5. The newly identified requirements can be accepted or rejected in consultation with software designer and the user. This is another kind of trade-off that can happen during the dissection of interface metaphor.

6.6 *Comparison Between Candidate Interface Metaphors*

It is possible to compare two or more candidate metaphors on the basis of various aspects and quantifiable attributes of interface metaphor introduced by us so far. Comparison between the 'classroom' and 'office' cabin metaphors used for Inscript Typing Tutor is presented below. Dissection of 'office cabin' metaphor is presented in Appendix E.

Table 6.13 Comparison between the candidate interface metaphors		
Parameters	**Classroom**	**Office Cabin**
Knowledge Dimensions	Day-to-day	Professional
Relational Class	Coherent	Coherent
Structural Category	*Multitudinous*	*Multitudinous*
Perspective	Children	Adults
Flavor and Tone	Colorful, playful, obvious	Less colorful, formal, subtle
Software Requirements	39	39
Cross-Domain Mappings (CDMS)	31	31
Conceptual Bandwidth	51	40
Usable Conceptual Bandwidth	31	31
Unmapped Concepts (UCs)	20 (40% of total)	9 (23% total)
Unmapped Requirements (URs)	8	8
Multitudinous	6	2
Inanimate Singleton	13	12
Animate Singleton	2	1
Flat Concepts	30	24

Both metaphors have produced somewhat identical mappings as they were tuned for the same software. This resulted in similar field of view, focus and usability requirements. User interface designer can compare the candidate metaphors and evaluate their potential on empirical basis. The comparison shown in Table 6.13 indicates that the 'classroom' metaphor has greater **potential** and **extensibility** from the perspective of Inscript Typing Tutor software.

Discussion

Relational classes, structural categories, the aspects of tuning and concept-by-concept dissection of interface metaphor all together have made it possible to quantify the metaphor. The new terminology of CDMs, UCs, URs, DT point, and usable conceptual bandwidth helps us in grasping and measuring the spread of the interface metaphor. We have provided various equations to establish the relationships and interdependence between these factors. **So far metaphors were treated as a topic of art and along came the spontaneity, intuition and subjectivity. But the theoretical basis developed so far has converted it into a systematic process. The documented outcome of dissection, and quantitative evaluation of interface metaphor, is useful to designers as well as software engineers, as the data is presented in objective terms.** The quantification of interface metaphor provides clear insights into the way the user experience of the software is shaping up.

Chapter 7. User and Application Domain Lexicons

In addition to the multimedia representations of interface metaphor, the verbal expression associated with each representation is extremely important for its comprehension by the users. The interface metaphor is reinforced by the associated proposition expressed in verbal form. The verbal expression can be effective only if it captures the vocabulary of specified users. Nielsen and Molich [1990] have proposed the usability heuristic as 'speak user's language' but they have not provided any process to achieve this goal. The method proposed in this chapter gives special attention to linguistic metaphors. The verbal expressions related to interface metaphors need to be treated differently, as they have to function in union with the multimedia representations. **Therefore, we propose to build User Domain Lexicon (UDL) and Application Domain Lexicon (ADL), to serve as a resource for designing the proposed linguistic metaphors.**

7.1 User Domain Lexicon (UDL)

After identifying the candidate interface metaphors using the techniques given in sections 3.1 and 3.2, it is necessary to capture the vocabulary of users associated with the selected interface metaphors. The vocabulary contains words and phrases that originate from the selected interface metaphors and the user domain. We call the collection of this type of vocabulary as User Domain Lexicon (UDL).

User Domain Lexicon (UDL) can be built simultaneously while the selection, tuning and dissection of interface metaphor go on. But it becomes a much more focused and simpler task after the interface metaphor is dissected. **Unmapped Requirements (URs) emerged after the dissection of interface metaphor can be represented using linguistic metaphors up to some extent.**

With reference to SDLC, the creation of User Domain Lexicon (UDL) happens during the stage of requirements elicitation. User interface designer has to perform following activities for building the User Domain Lexicon (UDL).

1. Record the narrations given by users about the processes to be computerized using a Dictaphone or any other audio / video recording devices.

2. Digitize the paper material such as printed forms, sample pages from registers, brochures, handouts and notable hand written comments and entries.

3. Take photographs or note down all intriguing textual references, which may have appeared on signboards, notice boards, posters and other sources visible in the premise of users. Digital camera or camera phone can be used for still photography.

4. Document the words and phrases related to the interface metaphor and the tasks performed by users.

Having finished the acquisition of various lexical sources, the user interface designer should -

1. Decompose the users' vocabulary in categories such as verbs, adjectives, nouns, technical terms, phrases and document them extensively.

2. Interact with users and find out the connotations, underlying concepts, and hidden meanings associated with the lexical acquisitions.

3. Investigate the mental models associated with the vocabulary.

4. Observe the application of user vocabulary in different situations.

7.1.1. Mental Models Associated with UDL

Mental model reveals the postulations associated with the words or phrases used by the users. It is possible to uncover the mental models through focused interviewing and discussions with users. It is very important to understand the difference between the definition of a word and the mental model associated with it. The definition of a word explains its standard meaning and the conceptual breakup; whereas, the associated mental model reveals the common pattern of understanding in terms of inferences, conclusions, interpretations, predictions, assumptions of users.

7.1.2. Discovering the Mental Model

One has to probe into the following aspects of all the lexical acquisitions in UDL. The mental model associated with a word or a phrase is revealed if the user interface designer finds answers to following questions.

- Who uses it?

- What does it convey to users?
- How other concerned individuals react to it?
- What experiences are connected with it?
- How much gravity or importance do they attach to it?
- How is it used in different situations?
- What assumptions are associated with it concerning quality, reliability, errors, and problems?
- In which script do they prefer to write the lexical acquisitions?
- What do they guess or infer about the status of a process when a particular word or phrase is used?
- What kind of abbreviations and colloquial terms do they use? (These terms need not be in one particular language. In Indian scenario, one finds mixed usage of English, *Hindi* and the regional languages in most states.) This investigation is more applicable if one is trying to localize the user interface.

This information expresses much more ground knowledge than the theoretical definition of a word used by users. It also captures the tacit knowledge of users.

7.1.3. Format for Documentation of UDL

Lexical acquisitions should not be arranged alphabetically. It is better to arrange them task wise or Cross-Domain Mappings (CDMs) and Unmapped Requirements (URs) wise. This reduces the chances of misuse due to superficial understanding of user vocabulary. The format for User Domain Lexicon (UDL) includes columns titled as Task or Cross-Domain Mappings (CDMs), words /phrases, Language/Script, Definition, Context of Application and Mental Model. Language/Script column includes information about language and the script in which users spell out a particular word. In the Mental Model column, one has to write the tacit meanings associated with a particular word or phrase. This attribute may or may not be applicable to all terms. Appendix F, Table F1. presents some examples of mental models discovered in the museum staff for the words like accession no., classify, comment, approve, sensitive, etc. for the digital library project of Prince of Wales Museum, Mumbai. The author of this dissertation carried out this experiment.

7.2 *Application Domain Lexicon (ADL)*

While preparing the user interface prototypes, several labels, titles and instructions are used as part of the buttons, dialog boxes and menus. This expression is usually full of technical terms related with software procedures. Most of these terms are part of the vocabulary of software development team. A collection of such terms is called as Application Domain Lexicon (ADL).

User interface designer prepares the Application Domain Lexicon (ADL) in the same format used for User Domain Lexicon (UDL). Technical procedures introduced in the software are likely to be different than the conventional procedures practiced by specified users. Therefore, the assumptions, dependencies, and constraints associated with the technical terms may be documented under the column of Mental Models. This represents the mental model of software development team. The format of User Domain Lexicon (UDL) can be used for documentation of Application Domain Lexicon (ADL) except for the Language/Script column, as it is not so much applicable. Refer Appendix F, Table F2. to see the sample of Application Domain Lexicon (ADL).

7.3 *Fusion of UDL and ADL*

Appropriate terms from User Domain Lexicon (UDL) and Application Domain Lexicon (ADL) have to be fused or replaced for designing the linguistic metaphors.

7.3.1. Traceability of Lexical Tradeoffs

Usually, verbal expressions used in the user interface are evolved in a very unsystematic manner. Authentic and reliable sources like User Domain Lexicon (UDL) and Application Domain Lexicon (ADL) are not available. Software terminology and unplanned mixture of words from user domain happens without any control. Building of User Domain Lexicon (UDL) and Application Domain Lexicon (ADL) can immensely benefit in controlling the fusion of two sets of vocabularies. The trade-offs between the two lexicons become easily traceable.

7.3.2. Conceptual Parallels Between ADL and UDL

It is possible to replace the software terms from Application Domain Lexicon (ADL) by the domain specific terms from User Domain Lexicon (UDL) for designing the linguistic metaphors. Terms from both lexicons having conceptual similarity may be juxtaposed to find the parallels.

Table 7.1 Fusion of ADL and UDL	
Application Domain Lexicon (ADL)	**User Domain Lexicon (UDL)**
Make an Executable	**Bind the Album**
As per the software developer, above feature does the following-	In the conventional album making process, binding an album conveys the following to the photographers and common users.
▪ It copies all linked files such as images, animations, audio clips into one folder.	▪ Completing the insertion of photographs.
▪ It copies required support files for running the application.	▪ Giving captions to pictures.
▪ It packages the application along with the viewer software.	▪ Covering the album with a decorative title.
▪ It allows the user to distribute the application on CDs.	▪ Packaging it for distribution and viewing by others.

Well-known types of linguistic metaphors such as ***similarity, entity and substance, orientation, personification, metonymy, similarity,*** etc. [Lakoff et al., 1980] can be discovered by juxtaposing the terms from Application Domain Lexicon (ADL) with User Domain Lexicon (UDL). The definitions and examples of these linguistic metaphors are provided in Appendix F1.3.

For example, QuickMM Album Author software used a phrase 'make an executable' which was replaced by 'bind the album'. Furthermore, even the name of software mentions 'Album'. This word immediately orients the users about what the software has to offer. See Table 7.1 for the break up of conceptual similarity between these phrases.

JATAN: Virtual Museum Builder has various modules that deal with administration, subscription, decision-making, data entry, etc. These are named as Admin. Register, Subscription Register, Decision Register, Data Entry Register. This is found immediately understandable and acceptable to the museum staff as they always deal with a variety of registers. The Admin. Register of JATAN allows managing the rights of users. It is titled as 'delegation of authority' as that is familiar to the higher authorities of museum. All these are ***similarity*** metaphors.

In the user interface prototype of JATAN, after finishing the data entry of a record it flashed a dialog as, 'this record is now accessible to curator'. Actually a record becomes accessible to curator from the database itself. It does not have to physically traverse from Data Entry Operator to Curator as in real life. But to give appropriate directional orientation to the users, the dialog is designed as 'the record is forwarded to curator'. In this case the comparison of Commentary of Task Performance (CTP) with Interface Play Script (IPS) became useful as given in Table 3.5 in chapter 3. Also when a record is commented by Curator or Director an instruction is displayed before the Data Entry Operator as 'a record has returned with comments'. In this case 'forwarding' and 'returning' are ***orientation*** metaphors.

'X number of records await your approval' is an example of ***metonymical*** metaphor. 'A record' or 'A register' are examples of ***entity and substance*** metaphors because they are addressed as entities when they are actually nonentities in the software.

In case of Inscript Typing Tutor, the interface prototype in Figure 9.6 shows play, pause, stop controls under the backboard window. These are used for viewing the animation clips that show how a particular letter is drawn. Play, pause, stop controls have appeared, as the software designer knew that the content would be presented in animation format. In the later stage it was changed into 'show me how to write', 'hold on', 'stop writing' type of tool tips. The author of this dissertation made these changes in order to comply with the 'classroom' interface metaphor. The idea is to give a feeling to the students that they are requesting the teacher.

Linguistic metaphors have always prevailed in software but no process was available to design them. Majority of linguistic metaphors in software are spontaneous creations but User Domain Lexicon (UDL) and Application Domain Lexicon (ADL) serve this purpose in a systematic manner.

Discussion

Creation of User Domain Lexicon (UDL) and Application Domain Lexicon (ADL) proposed in this chapter helps in braiding the user's and design models. The technique of juxtaposing both the lexicons provides the logical reasoning for deciding the names of features. It is also helpful in capturing the tacit knowledge of users. **Both lexicons could be shared over the network, for the common reference of software teams working across different geographic locations. This could prove very useful in offshore software projects.** User Domain Lexicon (UDL) especially can be useful beyond the confines of a software project. A software company can continue to enrich it if they are specializing in a particular market segment. **Thus the design process of linguistic metaphors proposed in this chapter brings completeness to the overall visualization of interface metaphor.**

Chapter 8. Usability Heuristics of Interface Metaphor

The HCI researchers have stated the need of defining the theoretical basis and evaluation method for the qualitative study of interface metaphors [Madsen, 1994] [Vaantinen, 1994] [Smilowitz, 1996] [Marcus, 1994, 1998]. 'Match between the system and real world', the well-known usability heuristic proposed by Nielsen and Molich [1990] suggests the application of real world metaphors. But it does not explain the heuristic criteria for qualitative evaluation of interface metaphor. **This heuristic is expanded further into 8 major criteria, 23 sub-criteria, and 41 Usability Indicators in the form of questions, for the usability evaluation of the interface metaphor. The eight heuristic criteria are named as** *Familiarity, Representability, Similarity, Extensibility, Compatibility, Co-operability, Cognitive Ergonomics and Feasibility.*

Numerous existing applications of interface metaphor are studied for evolving the criteria for heuristic evaluation. During this study, it was found that most applications of interface metaphor comply with only one or two heuristic criteria at a time out of the entire set defined in this chapter. This is due to unavailability of comprehensive theoretical basis for visualization of interface metaphor as stated above. Some of the insightful examples of interface metaphor are cited in Appendix G.

Some of the existing sub-criteria from the domains like semiotics, visual communication and cognitive psychology are incorporated as part the usability heuristics defined in this chapter and duly acknowledged. **The existing and newly identified criteria are presented in a structured manner to formulate a complete heuristic evaluation method for interface metaphor.**

In the following discussion, for some of the sub-criteria, 'multimedia rendering' is suggested as the 'basis for evaluation'. Multimedia rendering of interface metaphor is explained in Chapter 9. Basis of evaluation of every sub-criterion is indicated and acknowledged where other researchers have already contributed.

8.1 Usability Heuristics

All the **criteria, sub-criteria** and **Usability Indicators** mentioned in this section together are helpful in the qualitative evaluation and ensuring overall usability of interface metaphor for the proposed software. Each **Usability Indicator**[18] of every sub-criterion has been allotted maximum positive ratings of 3 points (High: +3, Medium: +2, Average: +1). Negative ratings (Low: -1, Bad: -2, Worst: -3) can also be applicable at the time of evaluation. Total maximum ratings for every criterion are also mentioned. Refer Section 8.2, Table 8.2 for more details of quantitative metrics for evaluating the merit of the interface metaphor.

The following sub-sections present the details of eight heuristic criteria namely Familiarity, Representability, Similarity, Extensibility, Compatibility, Co-operability, Cognitive Ergonomics and Feasibility.

---

[18] The pointer to a specific condition, which determines the usability

8.1.1.   Familiarity

Familiarity			
Sub-criteria	**Basis for Evaluation**	**Usability Indicators**	**Rating**
Existing Knowledge	Study of knowledge dimensions (Refer Chapter 3.)	1. Do the users have complete experience and knowledge of the reference domain selected as interface metaphor? Refer Appendix G1.1 for examples.	3
Perspective	Context study [Beyer, 1996]	2. Is the perspective of interface metaphor matching with the usual perspective of users towards the reference domain? 3. Does the reference domain have prominent and well-known identifiers (to the specified users) for its recognition? The perspective of users is defined by their position, needs and interests. The prominent identifiers include unique shapes, sizes, colors, textures, sounds, etc. Refer Appendix C1.1 for examples.	3 3
Generality	Study of knowledge dimensions (Refer Chapter 3.)	4. Is it common to most users in a stratified group? Generality signifies the applicability of interface metaphor to the entire class of users. Refer Appendix G1.2 for examples.	3
		Maximum Rating	12
The sub-criteria such as existing knowledge, perspective and the generality of reference domain are helpful in ensuring the familiarity of interface metaphor with users.			

8.1.2. Similarity

Similarity			
Sub-criteria	**Basis for Evaluation**	**Usability Indicators**	**Rating**
Structure	Dissection of Interface Metaphor (Refer Chapters 3 and 5.) Quantitative Evaluation (Refer Chapter 6.)	5. Is there natural similarity between the hierarchical order of concepts within the interface metaphor and software requirement? 6. Are there sufficient similarities between the clusters of software requirements and the conceptual clusters[19] in the interface metaphor? Refer Chapters 5 and 6 for examples.	3 3
Behavior	Dissection of Interface Metaphor (Refer Chapters 5.)	7. How much is the similarity between the needs served by the interface metaphor and the proposed software? 8. How much is the contribution of the affordances (interactive, behavioral and functional) of interface metaphor towards the usability of software? 9. How is the coverage of the traits of animate metaphor? 10. How much is the depth of the traits of animate metaphor? Refer Appendix G2.2. for examples. Refer Designing the Teacher Like Behavior of e-Learning System: A Case Study of Indian Scripts Typing Tutor [Katre, 2005]	3 3 3 3
Spatial Layout	Multimedia Rendering (Refer Chapter 9.)	11. Is the spatial arrangement (layout) of interface metaphor useful enough? 12. Is the spatial arrangement (order in time) of interface metaphor useful enough? Refer the examples given in Chapter 6. Refer Appendix G2.3 for examples.	3 3
		Maximum Rating	**24**

---

[19] Abstract ideas held together as a group.

Identification of similarities between the conceptual structure, behavior and spatial layout of interface metaphor; and the structure, functional behavior and arrangement of UI elements; helps in defining the Cross-Domain Mappings (CDMs).

8.1.3. Extensibility

Extensibility			
Sub-criteria	**Basis for Evaluation**	**Usability Indicators**	**Rating**
Unmapped Concepts (UCs)	Dissection of Interface Metaphor (Refer Chapter 5.) Quantitative Evaluation (Refer Chapter 6.)	13. Are there adequate *Unmapped Concepts (UCs)* available? 14. Are there many *Multitudinous Conceptual Structures* as part of *Unmapped Concepts (UCs)*? 15. Are the *Unmapped Concepts (UCs)* in line with the future scope of software? Refer Chapters 5 and 6 for examples.	3 3 3
Relevance & Longevity	User Participation [Dix et al., 2004] Context Study [Beyer, 1996]	16. Is the interface metaphor relevant in the social context? 17. Will it be relevant for adequate duration? Refer Appendix G3.1 for examples.	3 3
		Maximum Rating	**15**

Unmapped Concepts (UCs) emerged during the dissection of interface metaphor are helpful in estimating the availability of surplus concepts. The social relevance of interface metaphor for adequate duration helps us in ensuring its validity and longevity. Unmapped Concepts (UCs) and social relevance of interface metaphor both together define the extensibility of interface metaphor.

8.1.4. Compatibility

Compatibility			
Sub-criteria	**Basis for Evaluation**	**Usability Indicators**	**Rating**
Focus	Main functionalities and usability objectives of software (Refer Chapter 4.)	**18. Does it focus on the main functionalities of software?** **19. Does it focus on the usability objectives of software?** Refer Appendix C1.1. for examples.	3 3
Field of View	Software Scope, Dissection Termination (DT) Point, Terminus (Refer Chapters 4. and 5.)	**20. Is the field of view adequately matching with software scope?** Refer Appendix C1.2. for examples.	3
Customizability	The structure of interface metaphor and software requirements (Refer Chapter 5.)	**21. Can it be adjusted or modified to fit the requirements?** Refer Appendix G4.1 for examples.	3
		Maximum Rating	12
Focus, field of view and customizability of interface metaphor ensure its compatibility for the proposed software.			

8.1.5. Co-operability

Co-operability (Applicable in case of diverse interface metaphors)			
Sub-criteria	**Basis for Evaluation**	**Usability Indicators**	**Rating**
Conceptual Proximity	Analysis of interface metaphor (Refer Chapters 3 and 5.)	22. Are the core and supporting metaphors conceptually closer to each other or do they resonate with each other? There should be conceptual closeness between the core and supporting metaphors. They should not be completely disjointed or conveying contrary concepts. Refer Chapter 5. for examples.	3
Conceptual Alignment	Analysis of interface metaphor (Refer Chapters 3 and 5.)	23. Are the affordances of supporting metaphors enriching the conceptual structure of the core metaphor and serving the purpose? The supporting metaphors have to be converging in line with the core metaphor without disturbing its focus. Refer Chapter 5. for examples.	3
		Maximum Rating	6
Conceptual proximity and conceptual alignment ensure the co-operability of diverse interface metaphors.			

8.1.6.   Representability

Representability			
Sub-criteria	**Basis for Evaluation**	**Usability Indicators**	**Rating**
Appearance	Observations of Reference Domain / Objects	**24. Can the physical attributes be expressed through multimedia?** The interface metaphor has multi-sensory affordances like linguistic, visual, auditory, tactile, olfactory[20] and gustatory[21]. Among these, the visual attributes are very important, as they are most prominent in the perception of humans [Wade et al., 1991]. Visual affordances should be identified in terms of Form, Shape, Color, Texture, Patterns, Size, Overall Composition, etc. Refer chapter 7 for linguistic representation of metaphor and Appendix G5.1 for examples.	3
Depiction	Multimedia Rendering (Refer Chapter 9.)	**25. Is the approach of portrayal suitable? (Realistic or abstract)** **26. Does it address the visual literacy[22] [Katre, 2004c] of targeted users?** Depiction is about how the metaphoric representations are to be portrayed in terms of visual design, icons, animated clips, verbal (text), sounds and interactivity. Some metaphoric concepts are interesting but they are very difficult to portray. Refer Appendix G5.2. for examples.	3 3
		Maximum Rating	9
The attributes of appearance of the reference domain and the approach of depiction in terms of realistic or abstract portrayal decide the representability of interface metaphor.			

---

[20] Of or pertaining to the sense of smell.
[21] Of or pertaining to the sense of taste.
[22] The ability to effectively analyze and critically evaluate messages within a visual format.

8.1.7. Cognitive Ergonomics

Cognitive Ergonomics			
Sub-criteria	**Basis for Evaluation**	**Usability Indicators**	**Rating**
Mental Model	Commentary of Task Performance (CTP) (Refer Chapter 3.)	27. Is the selected interface metaphor capable of invoking the appropriate cognitive map of users? Refer Appendix G6.1 and I for examples.	3
Semantics	Analysis of Interface Metaphor (Refer Chapter 5.) Multimedia Rendering (Refer Chapter 9.) User Participation [Dix et al., 2004]	Are the semantic properties of a representation- 28. True? 29. Consistent (Unchangeable in the present context)? 30. Emphatic[23]? 31. Precise (Are there better alternatives)? 32. Does it convey the associated proposition effectively (the referent)? Semantics ensures the accuracy of representations [Marcus, 1993]. It is about the properties of a representation ascribed to the subject of communication. Refer Appendix G6.2 for examples.	3 3 3 3 3
Syntactic	Analysis of Interface Metaphor (Refer Chapter 5.) Multimedia Rendering (Refer Chapter 9.) User Participation [Dix et al., 2004]	33. Are all Cross-Domain Mappings meaningfully / logically arranged? 34. Does the design evolve rules that can be intuitively understood by the users? Syntactic is about forming combinations of visual attributes [Marcus, 1993] and a language out of signs. If one concept in the metaphor is understood by the users then the second and third can also follow. Refer Appendix G6.3 for examples.	3 3

---

[23] Assertion or emphasis of expression

Comprehensibility	Multimedia Rendering (Refer Chapter 9.)	35. Is the depiction of representation (the referred) recognizable to users?	3
		36. Do they correctly interpret the associated proposition (the referent)?	3
		Refer Appendix G6.4 for examples.	
Simplicity	Multimedia Rendering (Refer Chapter 9.)	37. Does the interface metaphor contribute towards the principle of economy?	3
		Refer Appendix I for examples.	
Recall	Multimedia Rendering (Refer Chapter 9.)	38. Do the attributes of appearance and spatial layout have mnemonic[24] potential [Katre, 2004c]?	3
		Refer Appendix G2.3 for examples.	
		Maximum Rating	36

Studying the mental model of users ensures the validity of the cognitive map vis a vis the interface metaphor. Semantic and syntactic conformance of design makes it comprehensible. The cognitive load is checked by the sub-criteria like simplicity of design and memory recall by the users. All these sub-criteria together ensure the cognitive ergonomics of the interface metaphor.

Cognitive ergonomics[25] [Sumner, 1997] is the new and specialized branch of research under the cognitive science domain [Barnard, 2000] [Boring, 2002].

Semiotics has already covered the evaluation of semantic and syntactic aspects in the past [Chandler, 1994] with greater focus on linguistic applications. We have retained these criteria as part of our heuristic evaluation method for completeness.

---

[24] A memory aid, an expression designed to be easier to remember.
[25] Cognitive ergonomics focuses on the fit between human cognitive abilities and limitations and the machine, task, environment, etc [Ergonomics Today, 2001].

8.1.8. Feasibility

Feasibility				
Sub-criteria	**Basis for Evaluation**	**Usability Indicators**		**Rating**
UI Constraints	Multimedia Rendering Feedback of software designer Quantitative Evaluation (Refer Chapters 6. and 9.)	39. Are the tradeoffs between the interface metaphor and UI constructive? 40. Are there adequate resources (time, finance, creative & technical skills) for design and development of interface metaphor? The software developer can assess the feasibility of UI implementation by observing the multimedia rendering. UI wizard of a programming tool has its own rules and restrictions with regard to usage of multimedia as part of the buttons, sliders, text boxes, tabs, picture boxes, etc. The size of application and memory constraints also need consideration. Refer Appendix G7.1 for examples.		3 3
Design Constraints		41. Are the tradeoffs between the interface metaphor and software design constructive? Software design process follows its own rules and has certain constraints that can hamper the overall development of interface metaphor. The design of software and the conceptual structure of interface metaphor can conflict with each other. The software and user interface designers should find such contradictions and work towards resolving them. Refer Chapter 6. for examples.		3
			Maximum Rating	9
Study of UI constraints and design constraints is helpful in ensuring the feasibility of the implementation of proposed interface metaphor.				

Feasibility criterion should not be mixed with other criteria while quantifying the total results as it mainly depends on resource availability. It does not evaluate any attributes of the interface metaphor.

Table 8.1 presents the criterion-wise maximum ratings (Number of Usability Indicators x 3).

| Table 8.1 Aggregate Score of Heuristic Evaluation ||
Heuristic Criteria	Criteria wise Maximum Ratings
Familiarity	12
Similarity	24
Extensibility	15
Compatibility	12
Co-operability	6
Representability	9
Cognitive Ergonomics	36
Feasibility	9

The co-operability criterion is applicable only in case of diverse interface metaphors. Next section provides the guidelines for the application of quantitative metrics. All the heuristic criteria together ensure the quality of overall user experience of the interface metaphor.

8.2   Quantifying the Heuristic Evaluation

8.2.1.   Converting the Grades into Points

It is possible to apply the quantification metrics presented in Table 8.2 for quantifying the results of the heuristic evaluation. Appropriate grades should be assigned by evaluating every Usability Indicator. The grades can be assigned in terms of **High, Medium, Average, Low, Bad** and **Worst**. Positive points are assigned to **High, Medium** and **Average** grades. Negative points are assigned to **Low, Bad** and **Worst** grades. The negative grades can be applied if the interface metaphor is complicating the software further and making it non-usable. Some criteria could be omitted from the evaluation if they are not applicable in certain application software projects. The grades can be converted into points for quantifying the merit of the interface metaphor. In the pre-rendering stage, one has to grade every Usability Indicator based on his/her best judgment. But the multimedia rendering of interface metaphor provides **objective basis** for grading.

Table 8.2 Quantification Metrics for Heuristic Evaluation	
Grade	**Points**
High	+3
Medium	+2
Average	+1
Low	-1
Bad	-2
Worst	-3
Not Applicable	NA

Tables 8.2 can be referred while quantifying the qualitative merit of the interface metaphor, e.g., if the reference domain is already part of the existing knowledge of specified users then it would be graded as **High** which translates into maximum rating of **3 points**.

Table 8.3 Quantified results of 'classroom' metaphor (pre-rendering)			
Criteria	**Max. Points**	**Points Earned**	**Approximate Percentages**
Familiarity	12	12	100%
Similarity	24	16	66%
Extensibility	15	12	80%
Compatibility	12	10	83%
Representability	9	6	66%
Cognitive Ergonomics	36	32	89%
Percentage of Usability			**81%**
Feasibility	9	6	**66%**
# Co-operability criterion is not applicable as the 'classroom' is a coherent metaphor.			

The percentage of feasibility is shown separately as it depends on the availability resources and technical skills. These factors vary depending on the project and the technical team. Feasibility criterion is very critical as even though the potential usability of interface metaphor is 80% as per the visualization, only 66% of it can be actually implemented due to feasibility constraints. Therefore the feasibility barriers must be overcome to exploit the full potential of interface metaphor.

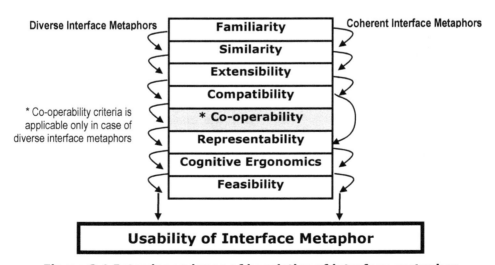

Figure 8.1 Interdependence of heuristics of interface metaphor

8.2.2.   Assigning Different Weightages to Heuristic Criteria

Quantification of heuristic evaluation presented in Table 8.3 gives equal weightage to all the criteria. It is possible that some software projects may not require to give same importance to all the criteria, e.g., the extensibility criterion may not be very important in all the software projects. In such case, the interface designer may like to give less weightage to extensibility criterion. In some projects, the representability criterion may require extra weightage compared to other criteria. The interface designer can assign additional value of weightage to each criterion while quantifying the final result of heuristic evaluation.

8.2.3.   Pre and Post Rendering Heuristic Evaluation

It is proposed to explore the design possibilities of interface metaphor by rendering it using interactive multimedia. The criteria of heuristic evaluation cannot be applied and tested unless the interface metaphor is rendered and given a tangible form. It is a significant effort. Therefore, the user interface designer is advised to carry out pre-rendering evaluation as shown in Table 8.3 before deciding to go for rendering. Heuristic evaluation in the pre-rendering stage is based on the visualization, experience and judgment of user interface designer. The interface metaphor is not taken up for multimedia rendering if not found satisfactory enough during the pre-rendering heuristic evaluation. Post-rendering heuristic evaluation of interface metaphor produces empirical results, as the fidelity of the multimedia rendering being much higher. This is a formative evaluation method as it generates feedback for further enhancement and allows the interface designer modify the design until the best results are achieved.

8.2.4.   Post Development Heuristic Evaluation

In the post-rendering and post-development stage the quality percentage of interface metaphor marginally drops if compared with the results of pre-rendering heuristic evaluation. It is because the sensory design of interface metaphor depends on various aspects, which are out of the scope of this dissertation namely the design skills of interface designer, the technical skills of software developer, team effort and adequacy of resources.

8.2.5.   Comparison of Usability Evaluation Methods (UEMs)

Researchers have not been able to provide direct and reliable comparisons between the Usability Evaluation Methods (UEMs), as there are no standard processes, definitions, criteria and metrics [Lund, 1998]. Some of the more popular expert-based UEMs include: Guideline Reviews based on interaction design guidelines such as those by Smith et al., [1986], Heuristic Evaluation [Nielsen et al., 1990], Cognitive Walkthroughs [Polson et al., 1990], Wharton et al., [1992] Usability Walkthroughs [Bias, 1991], Formal Usability Inspections [Kahn et al., 1994], and Heuristic Walkthroughs [Sears, 1997]. These UEMs are helpful identifying certain types of usability problems. Well defined processes, techniques and methods for the usability evaluation of interface metaphor are unavailable.

The visualization process of interface metaphor, proposed in this dissertation minimizes the risks and chances of making mistakes with interface metaphor. It is supported by a formative and analytical usability evaluation method. In fact, the application of the 8 broad criteria, 23 sub-criteria and 41 Usability Indicators provided by us is possible only if the visualization process is followed. The visualization process itself takes care of several usability aspects. **The 41 usability indicators are only for the purpose of verification and validation of interface metaphor. It also ensures the evaluation of minimum 41 unique usability aspects of interface metaphor unlike the other UEMs.**

Chapter 9. Multimedia Rendering and Usability Testing

9.1 Application of Interactive Multimedia

Hedberg et al [1992] emphasize the need of prototyping and evaluating the interface metaphors but they do not mention about how to design the prototypes and carry out the usability evaluation. **The multimedia rendering of interface metaphor proposed in this chapter bridges this gap.** This is likely to be mistaken as a new alternative of software prototyping. *But it is not so. It is the culmination of the visualization of interface metaphor. Unlike the low fidelity [Landy, 1995], medium fidelity [Rudd, 1996] and high fidelity prototyping methods [Cooper, 1994]; the approach of multimedia rendering completely focuses on the design of interface metaphor.* **Most software prototyping methods concentrate on simulating some part of functionality and rough outlining of user interface. These prototyping methods neither focus on functionality nor on user interface properly.** Furthermore, most of these are throwaway prototypes. **Whereas, the multimedia rendering proposed in this chapter, completely focuses on the design of interface metaphor. It produces several interface components in terms of graphics, layouts, animations and the scheme of interaction design that can be directly incorporated in the final software.**

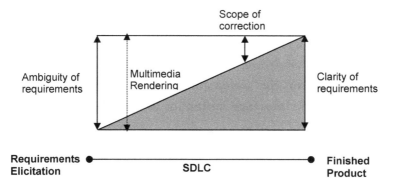

Figure 9.1   Scope of correction in SDLC

9.1.1.   Giving Tangible Form to Visualization

Interface metaphor design activity is interlinked with the software engineering process. It is a very demanding activity in terms of achieving certain quality of effect or 'user experience' through the rendering, as visualized by the interface designer. Not visualizing and planning it in advance can result in endless loop of refinement in software [Wilson, 1992]. Also modifying the software after it has been developed can be extremely costly and ineffective. As shown in Figure 9.1, the scope of correction is higher in the beginning of a project and it reduces towards the end. **Therefore, it is proposed to render the interface metaphor using multimedia in the formative stages of software design. It consolidates the outcome of visualization process. This process can be elusive unless it is not given a tangible and testable form. It permits the interface designer to explore several design possibilities and test the usability.**

9.1.2.   What Impedes User Interface Designers

High fidelity prototyping does fair justice to the functionality of software. Interface designers cannot contribute to the development of such functional prototypes as programmers dominate this activity. They are not expected to visualize the interface metaphor [McInerney, 2000]. Their prime focus is on achieving the desired functionality.

Another impeding factor is the handcuffed approach of software development. The programming environments like Visual Basic, JAVA, Visual C, C++, etc. have tied the GUI and programming together. The programmer has to invariably depend a lot on the standard GUI wizards at the time of coding. Due to this handcuffed approach, the user interface designers have to depend on programmers while implementing the design of interface metaphor [Katre, 2003]. **Therefore, user interface designers need a flexible medium for unleashing their creativity. They need to visualize and express the interface metaphor in their full capacity.**

9.1.3.   Availability of Technology and Technical Skills

Explorations of software prototyping so far are based on the constraints of 32-Bit operating systems such as Windows 95/ 98/ NT/ 2000 for the PC based users. **With the advent of Windows XP 64-Bit Edition, the applications are becoming richer in terms of innovative user interfaces and use of multimedia.**

Most user interface designers come from fine arts, visual communication, and multimedia backgrounds. They are generally conversant with multimedia tools and technologies like Adobe Photoshop, Macromedia Director, Macromedia Flash, Microsoft Power Point, Dreamweaver, HTML, Audio / Video Capturing and Editing. It is most appropriate to exploit these skills for rendering the interface metaphor.

The interface designers already use multimedia for user interface prototyping but they try to mimic the GUI components of the selected programming environment. This is unnecessary as the specialized UI prototyping tools [Landy, 1995] do the same. The UI prototyping tools help in prototyping the user interface layout and anticipating the functionality. They cannot help in design, rendering and testing of the interface metaphor. **Therefore, the capabilities of multimedia authoring tools can serve a unique purpose if they are utilized for rendering the interface metaphor.**

The discussion so far has presented the reasons of why the interface metaphor needs to be rendered using multimedia.

9.1.4. Objectives of Multimedia Rendering

Following are the objectives-

- Design and render the interface metaphor for the given software product.
- Ensure that all the heuristics of interface metaphor explained in chapter 8. are applied positively.
- Reveal the implementation issues related with interface design, interface programming, software design and technical feasibility.
- Uncover missed out and hidden software requirements.
- Test the usability of interface metaphor.
- Generate and incorporate user feedback on the design of interface metaphor.
- Share common understanding of proposed interface metaphor with the entire project team.

9.2   Multimedia Rendering

The candidate interface metaphor can be rendered using any type of multimedia authoring tools. The uniqueness of this activity lies in the integration of following artifacts / documents emerged out of the visualization process of interface metaphor presented in this dissertation.

| Table 9.1 Linking the Documents and Artifacts of Visualization Process with Multimedia Rendering		
Sr. No.	**Steps of Interface Metaphor Visualization**	**Artifacts / Documents**

1.	Selection of Interface Metaphor-
	   a. Common Knowledge Dimensions of Users
	   b. List of candidate interface metaphors
	   c. Juxtaposing of CTP and IPS
	   d. Classification based on interrelationships
	   e. Categorization based on levels of Conceptual Structure (CS)	

2.	Tuning of Interface Metaphor	
3.	Dissection of Interface Metaphor	
4.	Quantitative Evaluation of Interface Metaphor	
5.	UDL & ADL	
6.	Pre-rendering Heuristic Evaluation of Interface Metaphor	
7.	Quantified results of qualitative evaluation	

Following information may also be integrated as part of multimedia rendering for reference.

| Table 9.2 Standard UCD Documents and Artifacts		
Sr. No.	**Titles**	**Artifacts / Documents**
7.	Context Study	
8.	User Profile	
9.	Usability Objectives	
10.	Usability Requirements	
11.	Scanned Images of Paper Mockups (Low fidelity prototype)	

Under the link of context study, user interface designer can link important video clips, photographs and observations (indicated as ☉). Linking of specified documents and artifacts (📄 & 🖼 respectively) helps in anchoring the design decisions to the steps of visualization process. The design alternatives and evolutionary stages of interface rendering can be preserved (Refer Figures 9.3 to 9.8).

9.2.1.   Delineation of User Interface

User interface designer has to delineate the screen layouts in consultation with the team and the user. The delineated screens are then converted into measured layouts. Only after this stage the user interface designer can initiate the design and rendering of interface metaphor. It helps in separating both the schemes of user interface namely 'with' and 'without the metaphor'. An example is provided in Appendix H.

9.2.2.   Diffusion of Interface Metaphor

The diffusion of interface metaphor describes the gradation of rendering and depiction of interface metaphor in the software in terms of moderate, optimized, conceptual, behavioral / functional. As shown in Figure 9.2, user interface designer has to diffuse the rendering of interface metaphor gradually through minimum four levels as one interacts with the deeper levels of user interface.

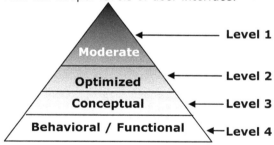

Figure 9.2 Gradual diffusion of interface metaphor

The outermost layer of user interface can have strong and obvious presence of interface metaphor. This is achieved through moderate rendering (refer Appendix J.) [Katre, 2002] of interface metaphor. The next level of interaction with software can have optimally rendered metaphors (refer Appendix J.) [Katre, 2002]. The third level can be conceptual and the fourth level is of purely behavioral / functional [Katre, 2005]. The levels of multimedia rendering mentioned here are very approximately defined and can be adapted based on the specific requirements of the product.

Figure 9.3 Multimedia Rendering integrated with documents / artifacts

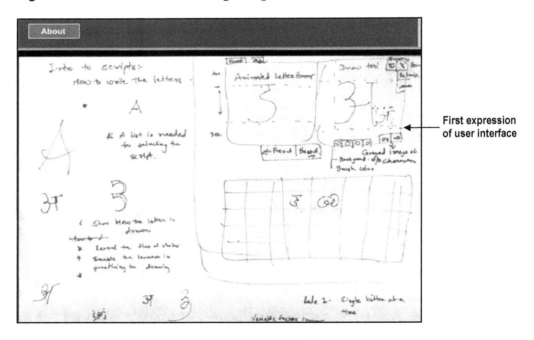

Figure 9.4 Digitized paper mockup

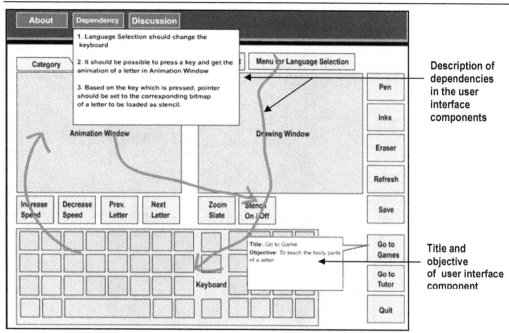

Figure 9.5 Delineation of initial layout of user interface

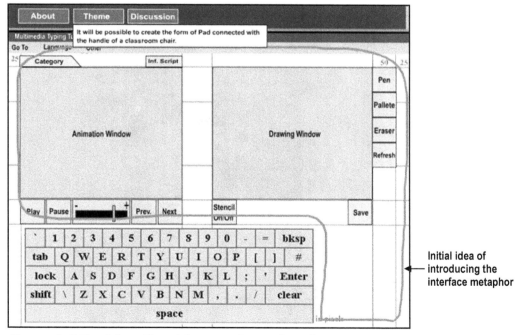

Figure 9.6 Most functional layout of user interface

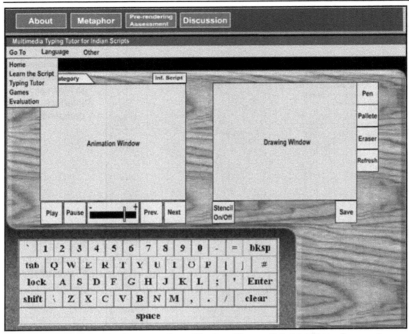

Figure 9.7 Rendering and optimization of interface layout

Figure 9.8 Final multimedia rendering of interface metaphor

9.2.2.1.   Functional User Interface Level

In this level, the functionality of software continues beyond the terminus of a branch of the conceptual structure. The metaphoric concepts are exhausted or terminated at this level. This level provides only the functional user interface.

The outer levels like moderate and optimized rendering of interface metaphor mobilize the intuitive faculty of users. By the time the user has reached the *functional* user interface level, (s)he is prepared to easily grasp the new functionalities of software.

9.2.3.   Interaction Design

So far we have seen how the interface metaphor can be interwoven with the structure, functionality, behavior and the user interface of software. It is possible to link various interface components rendered using multimedia for visualizing the interaction scenarios. The scheme of interaction is already part of the conceptual structure of interface metaphor, spatial layout and multimedia representations as shown in Chapters 5 and 6. Dialogs between the software and user can also be designed with the help of User Domain Lexicon (UDL) to enhance quality of interactivity.

9.2.4.   Usability Testing in Lab

The Usability Indicators of heuristic evaluation provided in Chapter 8. can be considered while rendering interface metaphor for achieving the desired qualities. Some of the criteria such as semantics, syntactic, comprehensibility, cognitive simplicity can be actually tested through user participation [Dix et Al., 2004]. Some examples of such usability tests are provided in Appendix I. The design of interface metaphor can be improvised based on the results of usability tests.

9.2.5.   Remote Usability Testing

We have designed a remote usability testing method for conducting the usability tests over a large sample of users from geographically distributed locations. **This method helps us in testing the comprehensibility and cross-cultural suitability of iconic representations. Refer Appendix J. for the details of this method.**

Thus the multimedia rendering of interface metaphor-

- **Integrates all the steps of visualization process proposed in this dissertation for quick reference.** It allows the interface designer, software developers and users to refer, compare, cross check and corroborate the linked information with the final rendered output. It provides basic interactivity and animation for sequencing the dialog boxes and illustrating different navigation scenarios.

- **Reveals hidden and missed out software requirements and usability problems.** Software designer is able to foresee the implementation issues and plan for them. **It maintains a record of all evolutionary stages of visualization along with the reasons of modifications.** User interface designer is able to fix several interface usability problems.

- **Develops common ground of understanding between the interface designer, software developers and the users.** It can be easily packaged and distributed through CDs and network for the teams operating from different locations. It encourages the participation of users in the process of interface metaphor design.

- **Produces certain interface components in terms of graphics, animations, layouts, structure, terminology and instructions that can be readily incorporated in the final software.** It helps in proper braiding of user's model, design model and software requirement.

- **Reduces the iterative changes in the software after it has been developed.**

Chapter 10. Integration with SDLC

10.1 *Integration of Visualization Process with SDLC*

As computers are moving from professional tools to consumer products, defining a process for design and integration of interface metaphors becomes most essential [Marcus, 1993]. Poovaiah [1994] has also highlighted the need of conceiving the design process of interface as a temporal process in terms of an interaction across time; as an organization of its various elements. The waterfall [Pressman, 2001] or spiral model [Boehm, 1988] of SDLC also do not present any defined steps for interface metaphor design. This has motivated us to integrate the visualization process of interface metaphor with the Waterfall Model of Software Development Life Cycle (SDLC) [Pressman, 2001]. We have provided separate figures for the selection process, the tuning process, and the entire process of visualization of interface metaphor.

The visualization process of interface metaphor is to be completed during the Requirements Engineering (RE) phase of SDLC. It has to be linked with the key activities of RE namely Requirements Elicitation and Requirements Analysis. The visualization process has to be finished just before Requirements Specification. It allows the software designer in incorporating the user interface specifications based on the multimedia rendering of interface metaphor. This becomes a very valuable input for evolving the design of software with full anticipation and plan for the proposed interface metaphor.

The SDLC begins with Requirements Elicitation activity [Pressman, 2001]. Several UCD activities such as Contextual Inquiry, Field Study, Structured Interviewing [Dix, et al., 2004], etc. also begin around same time. Unlike these general-purpose UCD methods, we have design the entire process with well-defined objectives.

10.1.1. Selection Process

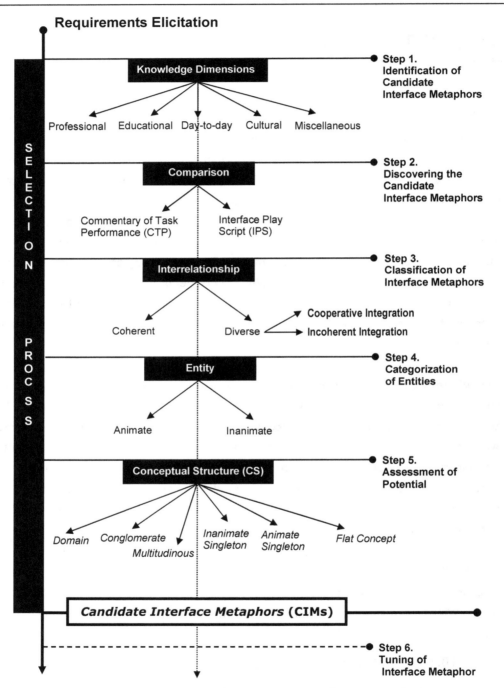

Figure 10.1 Selection of *candidate interface metaphors*

10.1.2.   Tuning Process

The user interface designer has to refer the planning documents of a software project for tuning the interface metaphor. Figure 10.2 shows the aspects of interface metaphor, which need to be tuned as per the respective determinants. The tuning of process of interface metaphor is explained in Chapter 4.

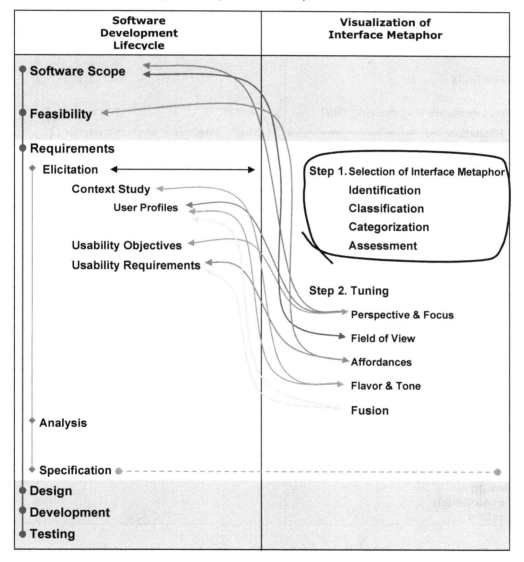

Figure 10.2 Tuning the interface metaphor

10.1.3. Entire Visualization Process

Figure 10.3 shows the entire visualization process of interface metaphor as part of the requirements engineering phase of SDLC. Analysis of interface metaphor is synchronized with the analysis of software requirements. Entire visualization process has to be completed before the requirements specification activity.

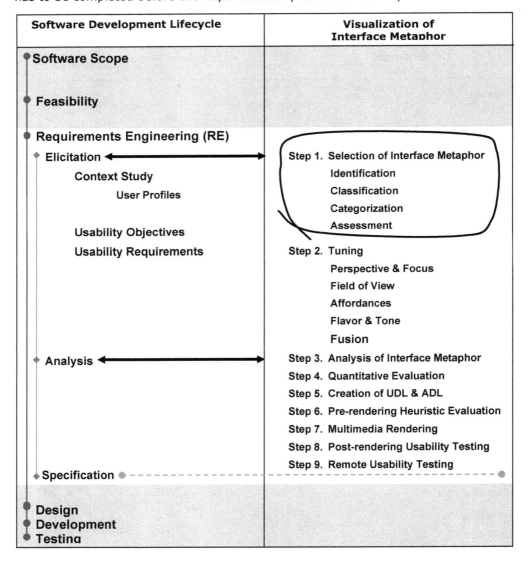

Figure 10.3 Visualization of interface metaphor as part of SDLC

The implementation of visualization process of interface metaphor is quite viable, as it does not demand special resource allocation. It is easily manageable within the general estimate of resources i.e. approx. 10% to 15% of the total resource requirements of the project [Baecker et al., 2000] for user interface design and usability testing activities. The resource requirements during the implementation of this process as part of two live projects are documented in Appendix K.

10.1.4. Applications

The process of visualization of interface metaphor proposed in this dissertation is useful for software applications that demand special attention to user interface design. These include Websites, Personal Computer Software; Multimedia Software for Education, Entertainment, Computer Games, Virtual Interactive Worlds; Application software dealing with Business, Digital Library, e-Governance; Productivity Software Tools; Public access systems on touch screen kiosks, Applications for mobile and other handheld devices like tablet etc. The execution of interface metaphor can be more expressive or subtle depending on the need of specified users.

The resource requirements required for implementing the proposed visualization process as part of two live projects are presented in Appendix K.

Conclusion, Major Contributions and Future Scope

Conclusion

The selection process of *candidate interface metaphors* is defined, which involves following major steps.

- Exploration of *candidate interface metaphors* based on common knowledge dimensions of users.
- Identification of *candidate interface metaphors* by juxtaposing the Commentary of Task Performance (CTP) and Interface Play Script (IPS).
- Classification of *candidate interface metaphors* based on their interrelationship.
- Categorization of *candidate interface metaphors* based on whether they are animate or inanimate entities
- Assessment of the potential of *candidate interface metaphors* based on different levels of conceptual structure

The comparative study of 'book' metaphor for identifying the variant aspects of interface metaphor given in Appendix C. and the respective determinants together provide objective basis for tuning the interface metaphor and resultant user experience. Such tuning is essential for satisfying the usability objectives and usability requirements of the software. The perspective, focus, field of view, flavor, tone and fusion of interface metaphor help in crafting the desired user experiences. The aspects of interface metaphor and the respective determinants are helpful in deciding the multimedia representations. The technical feasibility and usability requirements provide strong basis for selecting the affordances of interface metaphor and also in innovating the magical super-affordances. It helps in overcoming the real world constraints.

Dissections of Coherent, Diverse and *Animate* interface metaphors prove the possibility of concept-by-concept analysis of the underlying conceptual structure. It is possible to visualize the Cross-Domain Mappings (CDMs) and multimedia representation possibilities in advance. The dissection of interface metaphors is extremely helpful in identifying the gaps and missed out software requirements. It can complement the requirements elaboration activity. The dissection of interface metaphor provides an objective basis for estimating its coverage vis a vis to the software requirements.

The quantitative evaluation of dissected metaphor provides objective basis for estimating its coverage and extensibility. The shortage of metaphoric concepts can be estimated for identifying the suitable alternatives. In case of diverse interface metaphors, quantitative evaluation can help in maintaining the prominence of the core interface metaphor and thus maintain the orientation of software. The quantitative evaluation of *animate metaphor* is helpful in identifying the weaker traits of the software. Adding appropriate features and functionalities can strengthen them. It can also help in conceptualizing the behavior of software. The dissection of interface metaphor followed by the quantitative evaluation is helpful in anticipating the trade-offs between the software and interface metaphor. As a result, the user interface designer, software designer and the user together can regulate the trade-offs. Various parameters of quantitative evaluation help in the comparative analysis of *candidate interface metaphors*.

Creation of User Domain Lexicon (UDL) and Application Domain Lexicon (ADL) make the linguistic trade-offs traceable. The fusion of these lexicons is useful in designing the linguistic metaphors and capturing the vocabulary of users as part of interface metaphor design activity.

The usability heuristics involving 8 major criteria such as *Familiarity, Representability, Similarity, Extensibility, Compatibility, Co-operability, Cognitive Ergonomics and Feasibility*; fragmented into 23 sub-criteria; and 41 Usability Indicators are extremely helpful in evaluating the qualitative aspects of the interface metaphor. The heuristic criteria are very interdisciplinary in nature. The usability heuristics of interface metaphor are grounded in the steps of visualization process presented in this dissertation. For example, quantitative evaluation provides inputs for measuring the extensibility of interface metaphor. For every criterion, the basis for evaluation is specified. The quantitative metrics has been provided for quantifying the results of heuristic evaluation. Unlike the other heuristic methods, this one provides specific usability indicators and assures the evaluation of minimum 41 unique usability aspects of interface metaphor.

The multimedia rendering of interface metaphor consolidates all the documents, artifacts and the steps of visualization process. It helps in preserving the evolutionary stages of multimedia rendering, the decisions and the reasons of modifications. It helps in identification of missed out and hidden software requirements. It gives tangible and testable form to the visualization of interface metaphor.

The data produced through this process can be objectively defined and modeled to a large extent. The process of visualization is integrated with SDLC. The activities of requirements elicitation, analysis and specification can be synchronized with the identification, analysis and evaluation of interface metaphor. The user interface components and specifications are evolved through the multimedia rendering of interface metaphor. This helps in specifying the user interface requirements more accurately. This dissertation not only shows how the user's model, user requirements, and design model can be braided seamlessly; but also the synthesis of visualization and software engineering processes.

Diverse criteria from different disciplines such as software engineering, cognitive science, semiotics, linguistics, visual and multimedia communication are integrated in the evaluation process. These in togetherness form the usability heuristics of interface metaphor. The heuristics are very exhaustive, comprehensive, and practicable. However, the acceptance of interface metaphor design is largely experiential and dependent on the prominent trends in the feedback of specified users. The dissertation also provides a remote usability testing method for collection of feedback from users spread across diverse geographic regions.

Though it is not within the defined scope of this research, this work shows a path for design of HCI curriculum, specifically for interface metaphor design area. It also provides a new terminology that can be used only in the context of interface metaphor design, unlike the linguistic terminology being used so far. The new terminology defines and communicates the information that is useful in interface metaphor design activity. It also shows how the contributions from art and design professionals can be integrated in the engineering process.

Major Contributions

This dissertation has presented a comprehensive process for *visualization of interface metaphor* for software, which is helpful in designing interactive user interfaces with magical super-affordances and definitive user experiences.

It involves following important steps -

1. Selection process of interface metaphor comprising of following activities-

   a. Identification of candidate metaphors based on common knowledge dimensions and by juxtaposing the Commentary of Task Performance (CTP) and Interface Play Script (IPS)

   b. Classification based on interrelationships

   c. Categorization in terms of animate and inanimate metaphors

   d. Assessment of potential based various levels of conceptual structure

2. Tuning the aspects of interface metaphor as per the determinants for crafting the user experience

3. Concept-by-concept dissection of the interface metaphor for analyzing its conceptual structure and representation possibilities

4. Quantitative evaluation of interface metaphor

5. Creation and fusion of User Domain Lexicon (UDL) and Application Domain Lexicon (ADL) for formation of linguistic metaphors to be used in the user interface

6. Usability heuristics along with specific usability indicators for the qualitative evaluation of interface metaphor and the remote usability testing method

7. Multimedia rendering on the basis of inputs generated through the visualization process

8. Integration of the entire visualization process of interface metaphor with the Waterfall Model of Software Development Lifecycle (SDLC)

Future Scope

During the experiments and study of the problems presented in this dissertation, several new challenges for further research have surfaced. These have to be attempted separately, as the scope is very vast.

- The conceptual structures and representations of well-known or popular interface metaphors can be standardized. Templates of these interface metaphors could be designed.

- Requirements management tools can be extended further for documentation of interface metaphors and for the formation of Cross-Domain Mappings (CDMs).

- A software tool needs to be developed for mapping the User Domain Lexicon (UDL) and Application Domain Lexicon (ADL). User Domain Lexicon (UDL) can be made available over Internet or on CD at cost, for the software teams working in a similar market segment. User Domain Lexicon (UDL) can also be collectively enriched through a collaborative framework, which needs to be developed.

- It is necessary to study the gradual transformations in the mental models. A method needs to be evolved for capturing the stages of this transformation, and adjusting the interface metaphors to make up with the change.

- It is necessary to design effective and flexible tools for interface metaphor design. Options for decentralizing the interface design activity need to be explored so that it will be possible to design variety of user interfaces for the same product to address culture specific needs. It will no more be necessary to thrust the same user interface on all users. A library of culture specific rules for metaphoric representation can be identified. Cultural usability aspects of interface metaphor need to be defined.

APPENDICES

A. Study of Knowledge Dimensions

A1. Stratification of Users

Nos.	Name of Subject	Age	Education	Profession	Place	Lifestyle
	Table A1. Stratification of subjects for 3D Watershed Game Project					
1.	Chimaji Kodoji Avhad	65 years	2nd standard	Agriculture	Darewadi	Rural Maharashtrian
2.	Baapu Gahinath Ganage	28 years	7th standard	Agriculture	Ganagewadi	Rural Maharashtrian
3.	Mahadev Sudam	30 years	12th standard	Agriculture	Bid/Sangvi	Rural Maharashtrian
4.	Dilip Shivaji Gange	35 years	Illiterate	Agriculture	Ganagewadi	Rural Maharashtrian
5.	Ujwala Tanaji Lagad	34 years	9th standard	Agriculture	Vithekarwadi	Rural Maharashtrian
6.	Ramdas Shivaji Gange	35 Years	4th standard	Agriculture	Ganagewadi	Rural Maharashtrian
7.	Gorakh Shankar Gange	35 Years	Illiterate	Agriculture	Ashti	Rural Maharashtrian
8.	Gite Devidas Navnath	21 years	12th standard	Student	Lohasar	Rural Maharashtrian
9.	Raghunath Tukaram Wandekar	50 years	Illiterate	Agriculture	Lohasar	Rural Maharashtrian
10.	Padam Sawaleram Wandekar	35 years	Illiterate	Agriculture	Lohasar	Rural Maharashtrian
11.	Adinath Avhad	21 years	10th standard	Student	Lohasar	Rural Maharashtrian
12.	Bhagavan Sanap	38 years	5th standard	Agriculture	Lohasar	Rural Maharashtrian
13.	Ambubai Wandekar	60 years	Illiterate	Agriculture	Lohasar	Rural Maharashtrian
14.	Sambhaji Gite	36 years	Illiterate	Agriculture	Lohasar	Rural Maharashtrian
15.	Anjali Vaaghe	28 Years	M.S.S.	Teaching	Ahmednagar	Maharashtrian

Abovementioned subjects are briefly profiled to confirm the most common knowledge dimensions among the villagers from rural parts of *Maharashtra* state in India. It includes subjects from varied age groups, genders, and literacy levels. The professional and day-to-day knowledge dimensions are evidently most common to all. Cultural knowledge linked with religion is ruled out as every village in *Maharashtra* state has some percentage of different religions. **Right from the beginning, interface metaphors with only professional and day-to-day knowledge dimensions are explored for this project.**

A2. Professional / Educational Dimensions

C-DAC's National Multimedia Resource Centre has been conducting PG Diploma in Advanced Computer Arts program for over a decade now. Students and professionals have to qualify the Common Entrance Test (CET) for seeking admission to this course. In order to test the cognitive ability of students, the candidates are asked to elicit hierarchical structures of any given domains like university, film production, advertising agency, bank, etc. Every year, hundreds of students appear from various parts of India for the CET. The author of this dissertation himself has designed the CET papers and assessed hundreds of hierarchical structures for understanding the patterns of existing knowledge in the students. Some results of this assessment are presented here for substantiating the definition of knowledge dimensions and domains.

An architect who appeared for the CET conceived the hierarchical structure of the architecture department in a university, as shown in Figure A1. In this example, the candidate preferred to elicit the structure of architecture department only, as it is most familiar to him. He did not prefer to elaborate the activities of other departments that are less familiar to him. **We have seen many students giving the departmental breakup of a university and then elaborating the specific department where they studied. This is obviously a result of the professional/educational knowledge available with them.**

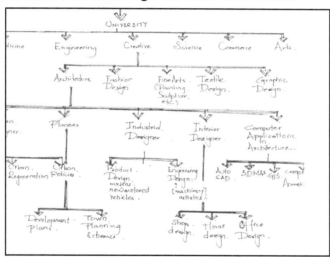

Figure A1. Hierarchical structure of a university defined by an architect

A3. Day-to-day Dimension

Figure A2. shows the hierarchical structure of a bank conceived by a fine artist who appeared for the CET. It is evident from the level of detailing that the candidate has very preliminary knowledge of banking. It is obvious that the person has used day-to-day Knowledge. A banker would have come up with a very detailed cognitive structure of banking operations; as for him it is part of his professional knowledge.

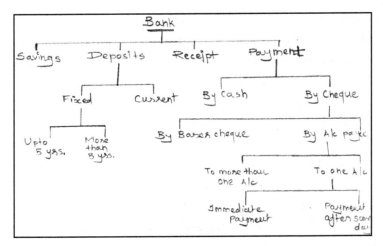

Figure A2. Hierarchical structure of a bank prepared by a fine artist

A4. Cultural Dimension

Figure A3. *Ganesha* metaphor used in *Dnyaneshwari* CD ROM

The spiritual metaphors rendered in *Dnyaneshwari* CD Title are understandable to *Hindu* devotees or people who are exposed to *Hindu* culture [Katre, 1999]. *Ganesha* metaphor, as the God of intellect and wisdom, is presented as shown in Figure A3. Variety of ancient philosophical scriptures is mapped with his body parts. The demonstrations of this CD Title in USA and UK by the author of this dissertation invoked a lot of curiosity among the westerners. But they could not follow the *Ganesha* metaphor as it being a culture specific representation.

The metaphors used in *Dnyaneshwari* CD ROMs are based on two knowledge dimensions simultaneously. The 'Book' metaphor was used for interface design and the spiritual metaphors are part of the main content of CD. They both belong to day-to-day and cultural knowledge dimensions respectively.

B. Example of CTP and IPS

B1. *Visualizing the Traversal of Record*

Figure B1 shows how the traversal of a record through In and Out Trays was visualized based on Commentary Task Performance (CTP) [Katre et al., 2004b]. To understand this figure one must know the underlying rules in the context of this application. They are as under.

- An unfinished record remains in the In Tray of Data Entry Operator (DEO).
- Only a finished or revised record goes to Curator.
- A finished record goes to Director after the Curator has checked it. The Curator can comment and return it to DEO for corrections.
- DEO resends it in a revised form.
- Director approves a record checked by Curator.
- An approved record becomes part of Main Accession Register.

DEO's In Tray	DEO's Out Tray
Unfinished records	Finished Records
Records commented by Curator	Finalized Record
Records commented by Director	

Curator's In Tray	Curator's Out Tray
Finished records	Checked Records
Revised records	Records Commented by Curator
Records commented by Director	
Finalized Records	

Director's In Tray	Director's Out Tray
Checked Records	Records commented by Director
Finalized Records	Approved Records

Main Accession Register	
Approved Records	

Figure B1. Traversal of a record through In and Out Trays

At this stage In and Out Trays metaphor was confirmed. This metaphor is integrated at conceptual level in the design of software.

C.   Variant Aspects and Determinants of Variance

It is observed that the same interface metaphor is applied differently in different software products. Although it is the same metaphor, it highlights different similarities with the software; it also produces different images and quality of experience [Madsen, 2000]. We have realized that it is a result of the way the interface metaphor is tuned. What are the aspects of this tuning? And how to determine whether an interface metaphor is properly tuned for the given software application? In order to find answers to these questions, a common interface metaphor and its applications in different software products are examined. This study is documented here.

The popular 'book' metaphor, which has been widely exploited by user interface designers, is selected for this purpose. The software manifestation of 'book' metaphor has been in terms of E-books [Nielsen, 1998] [Shiratuddin, 2003], Virtual Books [Chu, 2004] [Card, 2004], interactive multimedia CD Titles (referred as Multimedia Books) and interfaces of variety of other software applications. The book metaphor has also shaped hardware gadgets like PDAs, Notebooks and other portable devices [Press, 2000] [Wilson, 2001]. There have been extensive deliberations on the issues of look & feel aspects and usability of 'book' metaphor [Russell, 2001] [Wilson, 2002]. During this study the intention is not to evaluate the applications of 'book' metaphor but to find the aspects of this metaphor that have varied and the reasons behind it.

Several research publications presenting detailed case studies of 'book' metaphor are studied for this purpose. The hardware devices for book reading are not included in this study. Wherever possible, the actual software products were used for experiencing the user interface.

The 'book' is referred as the central point of discussion. Element level of metaphors starting from something as basic as 'paper' up to the collection of books in the form of 'library' are also considered. Different genres of books are also considered for identifying their impact on interface design.

C1. Comparison of Variance in Interface Metaphor

The applications of 'book' metaphor are presented in the order of progression such as a page, a physical book, e-book publishing and distribution, a multimedia book, a book as part of the classroom, a pile of books/documents/files, a library, a spiritual book and an e-book for legal research. Appropriate examples are cited under each category and the metaphorical features of the products are enlisted. Features of multiple products are combined together in some categories for avoiding the duplication of similar features.

Table C1. Applications of 'Book' Metaphor		
Metaphor	**Products**	**Metaphorical Features**
Page	Magic Pages [Götze, 2003]	<ul><li>Filters for extracting the contents based on their attributes</li><li>Showing annotations based on the type of pen, color of ink</li><li>Transparent layers of a page</li></ul>
Physical Book	3Book [Card, 2004 a. and b.] British National Library's 'Turning the pages' project [Chu, 2004]	<ul><li>A virtual 3D book with realistic physical appearance</li><li>Binding axis</li><li>Changing thickness of the book on both sides of the binding axis as one turns the pages</li><li>Page turning effect</li><li>Zoom In and Out</li><li>Bookmarks</li></ul>
e-Book Publishing and Distribution	Acrobat Reader (Henke, 1998) Dynamic WAIS Book [Bizzozero, 1994] Zinio Book Reader	**More or less common features of most e-book publishing tools**<ul><li>Index</li><li>Next, Previous Page</li><li>Bookmark</li><li>Annotation</li><li>Notes</li><li>Text Highlight</li><li>Rotate Pages</li><li>Article Tool</li><li>Touchup Text</li><li>Pencil</li><li>Distribution over network</li><li>Standard page turning effect</li><li>Highlight tool</li><li>Rotate Pages</li><li>Extract Pages</li><li>Import Pages</li><li>Page Layouts</li><li>Zoom In/Out</li><li>Print</li><li>Building a collection of books</li></ul>
Multimedia	Listen Reader	**Listen Reader**

Book	[Back, 2001] *Kumar Vishwa Kosha* CD Title Life & Work of *Ramanujan* CD Title	<ul><li>Electronically augmented paper based audio book</li><li>Invokes multi-layered movie sound track as one handles a real book</li></ul>**Kumar Vishwa Kosha**<ul><li>Alphabetical Index in *Marathi*</li><li>Audio/Visual/Video Index</li><li>Multiple Pages</li><li>Next, Previous Page</li><li>Print</li><li>Bookmark (Folded corner of a page)</li><li>Magnify Image</li></ul>**Life & Work of *Ramanujan* CD Title**<ul><li>Similar set of features as above</li></ul>
Book in a classroom	Inscript Typing Tutor for Indian Scripts	<ul><li>Index</li><li>Multiple Pages</li><li>Next, Previous Page</li></ul>
Pile of books	Pile Interface [Mander, 1992]	<ul><li>Browsing through a pile of files, documents, books</li><li>Piles of mixed media</li><li>Categorization based on attributes of contents</li><li>Spread out piles</li><li>Pile structure</li><li>Side shift</li><li>Pulling out a document</li></ul>
Books and book shelves (Personal collection)	KeeBook Creator for Education [Shiratuddin, 2003]	<ul><li>Select book jacket</li><li>Full book view</li><li>Page view</li><li>Book stand</li><li>Book shelves</li><li>Shelf name for topic wise categorization of books</li></ul>
Library	Digital Library [Dunker, 2002]	<ul><li>All book related concepts in addition to classification, cataloging, sharable annotation, dictionary, intelligent searching and library management features</li></ul>
Book as a Temple (Spiritual Book)	*Dnyaneshwari* CD Title [Katre, 1999]	<ul><li>Next, Previous Page</li><li>Auto-playing of audio recitation along with auto-page turning</li><li>Meanings of difficult words</li><li>Time for practicing the recitation of verses during auto-play mode</li><li>Jump to a Verse</li><li>Resume from the point where stopped last time</li><li>Show only *Bhagvadgita* or *Dnyaneshwari* or both together</li><li>Bookmark (Peacock feather)</li><li>Store multiple bookmarks</li></ul>

		<ul><li>Annotation (Office clip)</li><li>Status of location in book</li><li>Devine foresight for viewing the rendering of spiritual metaphors</li><li>Print</li></ul>
e-Book for Legal Research	Xlibris [Marshall, 2001]	<ul><li>Annotations</li><li>View annotated passages</li><li>Clipped passages</li><li>Thematic organization of passages</li><li>Linking, cross-referencing</li></ul>

Above documentation reveals that user interface designers have viewed the 'book' metaphor from different viewpoints and emphasized on different elements of it. The following discussion presents the comparative analysis of varied applications of 'book' metaphor enlisted in Table C1.

C1.1. Perspective and Focus

- The functionalities of Acrobat Reader are centred on electronic publishing, distribution and reading of documents over network. It is designed to publish electronic user manuals, technical documents and research publications for professionals. This has resulted in greater detailing of access restriction through features like digital signature, self-sign and reading tools for annotations, notes, highlighting and touch up, etc. All features are oriented to satisfy the publishers and readers of technical literature.

- Inscript Typing Tutor mainly focuses on 'classroom' metaphor. 'Book' is one of the many objects in the classroom. The application does not deal so much with reading material and therefore there is no focus on 'book' metaphor. The 'book' is merely an icon as part of the classroom. The software is designed for school children.

- The 3book project focuses on achieving physical look and feel of the book. The realistic page turning effect is the most attractive functionality of 3Book. The book can also be rotated in 3d space for the convenience of reading. 3Book is designed for general readers.

- The 'Pile' metaphor focuses on how it can be used for organization of documents in an operating system. It does not focus on the contents of documents. It has been designed for general computer users.

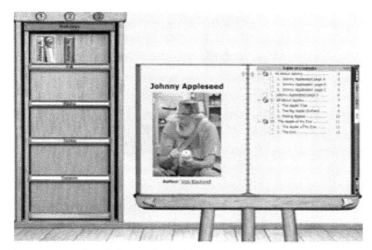

Figure C1. KeeBook with Bookshelf, Book Jackets and Reading Stand

- KeeBook software focuses on features that are based on bookshelves, styles of book jackets and book stand for reading unlike any other product. It is targeted to enable the readers in managing a personal collection of e-books. It also supports the choice of book jackets and the freedom to arrange the books in the shelf.

These observations clearly indicate that the perspective and focus of 'book' metaphor has varied in every example. In all these examples the targeted users, usability objectives and the importance attached to certain functionalities is distinctly different.

C1.2. Field of View

- It can be observed that the field of view has varied starting from 'page' to 'library'. It is like zooming out starting from an element level up to the environment level. Field of view is particularly different in Magic Pages, *Dnyaneshwari*, Inscript Typing Tutor, Acrobat Reader and Digital Library applications.

- In case of Magic Pages, the field of view is very narrow and it includes the attributes of a page and information content printed on it.

- Inscript Typing Tutor is based on 'Classroom' metaphor. The book is one of the several elements of 'classroom' as seen in Figure C2. Therefore, it does not include most of the characteristics of a book. It serves only as a link for giving introductory information about the script chosen for typing.

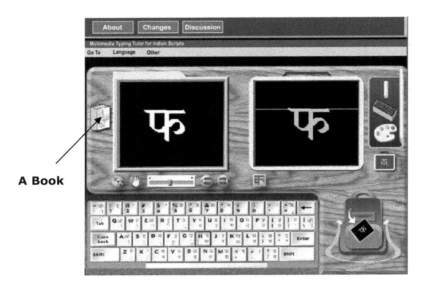

A Book

Figure C2. 'Book' as an element of 'classroom' metaphor

- Keebook software keeps books, bookshelves and bookstand are kept in the field of view.
- Acrobat Reader includes several activities relating to publishing, distribution and reading of documents.
- The digital library includes books, shelves, catalogs, librarian and a host of other features relating to sharing of books over network. In case of Acrobat Reader and Digital Library the field of view is much wider.

It is evident from the above examples that the field of view of 'book' metaphor has got widened or narrowed to match with the scope of software.

C1.3. Affordances

Usually only those affordances of metaphor get selected [Mohnkern, 1997] [Norman, 1990 and 1999] [Torenvliet, 2003] that help in satisfying the usability requirements.

- For example, Acrobat Reader dwells upon the affordances of 'book' metaphor such as annotations, pagination, page layouts, bookmarks, highlighting tool, etc. *Dnyaneshwari* does not include all these features. But it has some other features like auto-play where pages turn automatically and the verses are recited. It also provides meanings of difficult words.
- The concept of clipping and indexing of annotated passages has appeared only in e-book for legal research and not in any other application.

- Sorting of annotations on the basis of ink color is supported only in Magic Pages.

- Support for selecting the book jacket and bookshelves for managing the personal collection of books is unique to KeeBook Creator.

- Audio support of Listen Reader is not provided anywhere.

- The realism of page turning and realistic appearance is attempted only in 3Book project.

The usability requirements and feasibility constraints are unique in all the examples mentioned here. These have determined the selection of affordances of 'book' and related metaphors.

C1.4. Flavor & Tone

- The multi-layered sound track of Listen Reader offers different background music and sounds for setting appropriate ambience while reading a story from the book. Basically it adopts appropriate flavor of the story. The tonal quality is decided based on whether the stories are for children, teenagers or adults.

- The representation of 'bookmark' concept has varied in different products as shown in Figure C3. *Dnyaneshwari* CD Title uses 'peacock feather' as a bookmark, whereas *Kumar Vishwa Kosha* folds the top-right corner of a page.

- *As* shown in Figure C4., the 'Exit' icon in *Dnyaneshwari* is represented by a picture of a religious book being wrapped in a saffron cloth. *As Hindu* devotees have a tradition of wrapping the religious book in sacred saffron colored cloth after they have finished reading it. This representation contributes to the spiritual flavor of application.

- If Figures B2. and B5 are compared they show a distinct difference in the flavor and tonality of user interface of Inscript Typing Tutor. It is designed to offer different experience to school children and adult users. Therefore, Figure B5. shows smaller icons, conservative colors and representations of electronic gadget, executive notepad and folder in place of backboard, slate, toolbox and schoolbag from the classroom.

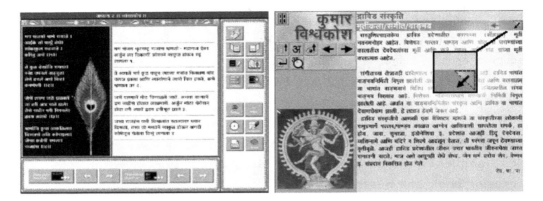

Figure C3. Bookmark Representations

Figure C4. Exit Button in *Dnyaneshwari*

Figure C5. Inscript Typing Tutor for Professionals

The distinct change in flavor and tone of interface metaphor is due to the context and the role of software.

C1.5 Fusion

- The real life affordances like the physical look and feel, page turning effect, changing thickness of the sides as the pages get turned, stacking the books in cupboards or shelves are fused with the software for offering real world experience.

- As one turns the pages in *Dnyaneshwari*, one can listen to the recitation of verses on that particular page. The recitation of verses is not the affordance of a regular book. It is the affordance of a scholar of *Dnyaneshwari.* But it is fused with the book metaphor in *Dnyaneshwari.*

- Another example is of MS Word where the affordance of a dictionary is fused with the typewriter metaphor to provide automatic spell checking.

Following are the examples in which the constraints from real life are overcome.

- In auto play mode, the pages turn automatically and the recitation of verses continues along with it for around 240 hrs.

- The divine foresight feature in *Dnyaneshwari* CD Title enables you to see the animated visualization of spiritual metaphors.

- The possibility of searching by keyword in Acrobat Reader, sorting the annotations based on ink colors in Magic Pages or automatically clipping and indexing the annotated passages in e-book for legal research are the other examples of magical effect.

Most of the above mentioned magical effects are achieved during the effort of meeting the aspirations of users and usability requirements. This comparative analysis has helped us in identifying the aspects of interface metaphor and the respective determinants used for their tuning. The same 'book' metaphor is tuned differently for different software products.

D. Preparing to Dissect the Interface Metaphor

D1. Selection and Tuning of 'Classroom' Metaphor

Table D1. Selection of Interface Metaphor for Inscript Typing Tutor	
Software Product	Inscript Typing Tutor for Indian Scripts
Users	Schoolchildren Age Group: 6 to 15 years Country: India
Most common knowledge dimension	Day-to-day Knowledge
Knowledge domain	School
Reach	Global
Localization	Very small percentage
Juxtaposing of CTP and IPS	Not Applicable
Interface metaphor identified	Classroom
Knowledge dimension of metaphor	Day-to-day Knowledge
Matching of knowledge dimensions	Positive
Possibility of comprehension	High
Category based on interrelationships	Coherent
Category based on the levels of conceptual structure	*Multitudinous CS*
Potential of Interface Metaphor	High
Decision	**Selected**

Table D2. Tuning of Interface Metaphor for Inscript Typing Tutor	
User School Children	**Perspective** View the classroom from the standpoint of school children.
Usability objectives ▪ Inscript keyboard is difficult to learn. Proposed typing tutor software should teach the Inscript keyboard without any overhead of learning for mastering its own user interface. ▪ Learning process of typing in variety of Indian Scripts, using Inscript keyboard should become a playful activity.	**Focus** ▪ Classroom environment is very familiar to schoolchildren. It allows incorporation of lessons, exercises and tests. To make it enjoyable it will be possible to introduce games, puzzles and quiz type of activities. ▪ Most important functionalities of Inscript Typing Tutor like learning to write Indian scripts and practicing to type with increasing complexity can be evolved into a well-planned course. This course is proposed to be delivered in the most familiar classroom environment. ▪ Metaphoric concepts like blackboard, slate, notebooks, books, toolbox, schoolbag, teacher, test, mark sheet, certificate can be kept in focus.

Software Scope The scope of software is briefly defined as under. Inscript Typing Tutor should- - Teach how to write Indian scripts. - Teach how to type using Inscript keyboard and help in developing the typing skills in a particular Indian script. - Provide alphabetical games and puzzles to make the typing lessons enjoyable. - Evaluate the typing performance of the learner and provide a mark sheet. It should also provide a certificate after successful completion of the course. -	**Field of View** - Keeping just the classroom activities in the field of view should be sufficient. Activities relating to entire school need not be considered immediately.
Usability Requirements - The user should feel that (s)he is sitting in the classroom. - Writing in Indian scripts should be as good as regular pen and paper experience. - Tutor should show how to write the alphabet. - Tutor should guide and help while learning to type. - The software technology look should be invisible.	**Affordances** - Visual look and feel of classroom. - Real life behavior of objects wherever they are useful in meeting the usability requirements.
Context - Educational	**Flavor** - A mix of educational and yet very entertaining flavor for children.
Role of Software - To teach how to type in Indian Scripts	**Tone** - The tone of teaching should address the ego state of schoolchildren. The software should enforce discipline while learning and at the same time hold the interest of school children.
User Aspirations - Typing using Inscript keyboard is perceived as very difficult due to natural choice of English for transactions. Can it be made simpler? - Learning to type in Indian scripts is quite boring. Can it be interesting? - In case of non-resident Indians, who can teach us?	**Fusion** - It is not the job of tutoring software to simplify typing using Inscript keyboard. All it can do is make the skill development process enjoyable. - Weaving the typing games, puzzles, lessons, exercises and tests as part of a course to make it interesting. - Provide classroom environment to maintain educational flavor. - Teach through lessons, exercises, dialogs and provide guidance to learners. - Support auto evaluation of typing, production of mark sheet and finally the certificate to create magical effects.

D2. Selection and Tuning of Diverse Metaphors

Table D3. Selection of Interface Metaphor for Quick MM Album Author	
Software Product	QuickMM Album Author
Users	Photographers and ordinary People from India
Most common knowledge dimensions	Professional, Day-to-day
Knowledge domain	Photography
Reach	Global
Localization	Event specific
Juxtaposing of CTP and IPS	Done (Results given below)
Core metaphor identified	Photo Album
Supporting metaphors	Exhibition, Greeting Card, Calendar
Knowledge dimensions of metaphor	A mix of professional and day-to-day
Matching of knowledge dimensions	Positive
Category based on interrelationship	Diverse
Category based on conceptual structure	**Album:** *Inanimate Singleton* **Exhibition:** *Conglomerate* **Greeting Card:** *Inanimate Singleton* **Calendar:** *Inanimate Singleton*
Potential of Interface Metaphor	High
Decision	**Selected**

Table D4. Tuning of Interface Metaphor for Quick MM Album Author	
User Photographers and ordinary (in terms of skills, education, economic status) people from India	**Perspective** From photo album to multimedia album production
Usability objectives ▪ Enable photographers and ordinary people from India in authoring a multimedia album without requiring them to learn lingo scripting or programming.	**Focus** ▪ Making an album of photographs is well known to all users. Therefore focus should be on producing a multimedia album. ▪ The supporting metaphors like exhibition, greeting card and calendar should not be given so much prominence
Software Scope ▪ Provide a readymade template for integration of multimedia contents. ▪ The template should address the requirements of event documentation. The multimedia contents will be in terms of photographs, video clips, audio clips, etc. ▪ Provide a library of theme based background images, cliparts ▪ Support of Indian languages for giving captions	**Field of View** ▪ Keeping just the album metaphor in the field of view is not adequate as there are many other requirements beyond the affordances of album.

Usability Requirements	Affordances
▪ The process should be just like integrating an ordinary photo album ▪ The user should be able to predict the functionalities ▪ No scripting/programming	▪ Most of the real life affordances of a photo album like insertion of photos, pages, thematic colors, images for cover design, etc.
Context	**Flavor**
▪ Authoring: Photo album production ▪ The resultant application: personal taste, event to be documented	▪ Authoring: Photo album production ▪ The resultant application: tune to the flavor of the event of documentation such as marriage, inaugural function, etc.
Role of Software	**Tone**
Facilitate the process of multimedia album production	Neutral
User Aspirations	**Fusion**
▪ Exploit computers to add value to their existing profession ▪ Provide multimedia albums to their customers	▪ Integrating video, audio clips along with photographs, as part of an album is quite magical. The affordances of exhibition, greeting card, calendar should be fused with album metaphor

It is important to know why exhibition, greeting card and calendar metaphors are not kept in focus. Exhibition is a *conglomerate metaphor* but if you dissect it deeper, it produces concepts that have no relevance with the software scope of QuickMM Album Author. Concepts like venue, stalls, space allocation, seminars, panels, reception, sponsors, advertisements, etc. have no conceptual alignment with Album metaphor. Therefore, it is treated as a *flat metaphor*. Whereas, greeting card and calendar are *inanimate singleton metaphors*. Their conceptual structure is naturally less rich than that of the album metaphor.

E. Dissection of Office Cabin Metaphor

Table E1. Dissection of 'Office Cabin' as Interface Metaphor for Inscript Typing Tutor Software					
Cross Domain Mappings (CDMs)					
CDM Nos.	Req. IDs	Application Domain *Requirement Titles*	Reference Domain *Office Cabin*	Meta. Cat.	MM Rep.
CDM 1.	1.	Introduction to Indian Scripts	Book	IS	L, V
CDM 2.	2.	Demonstrate writing	Palmtop (Modern device)	F	L, V
CDM 3.	3.	Drawing area for practice	Executive Notepad	F	L, V
CDM 4.	4.	Reference of letter (on/off)	Tracing paper (add/remove)	F	I, V
CDM 5.	5.	Draw tool	Executive class Pen	IS	I, Fn,
CDM 6.	6.	Erase drawing	Eraser	F	IP, I
CDM 7.	7.	Refresh	New blank page	F	I
CDM 8.	8.	Typing speed	Electronic watch	F	I, V
CDM 9.	9.	Open drawing	Taking it out from the folder	F	IP, An
CDM 10.	10.	Authentication of certificate	Signature of Examiner	F	V, T
CDM 11.	11.	Save current state of work	Hold it until I clear	F	IP, Fn
CDM 12.	12.	Provide guidance & tips	Professional colleague / mentor	AS	-
CDM 13.	13.	Register User Name	Joining the Indian Language Club	S	Fn, I
CDM 14.	14.	Save settings (slate, pencil, color)	Noting it in personal diary	F	L, I, IP
CDM 15.	15.	Save my typing / writing	Keeping it in a exec. suitcase	F	IP, An
CDM 16.	16.	Show demo and drawing area	Palmtop and notepad	F	IP, L
CDM 17.	17.	View demo only	Mentor only (Palmtop)	F	IP, L
CDM 18.	18.	View my drawing area only	Member only (Notepad)	F	IP, L
CDM 19.	19.	Build letter forms with components	Puzzle / Game /Quiz	IS	-
CDM 20.	20.	Visual Key pressing by mouse	Key pressing sound	F	A
CDM 21.	21.	Warning signal	Beep sound	F	A
CDM 22.	22.	Performance evaluation	Mark sheet and Certificate	IS	L
CDM 23.	23.	Tools	Executive Toolset	IS	IP, L, I
CDM 24.	24.	Log maintenance	Attendance Register	IS	Fn, V, L, I

Table E2. Unmapped Concepts (UCs) of 'office cabin' as interface metaphor				
Application Domain *Requirement Titles*	**UC Nos.**	**Reference Domain** *Office Cabin*	**Meta. Cat.**	**MM Rep.**
	UC 1.	Phone / Fax	?	?
	UC 2.	Library	M	M
	UC 3.	Notice Board	S	L, Fn
	UC 4.	Dictionary	S	Fn
	UC 5.	Indian script e-mail	S	Fn
No Matching Requirements	UC 6.	Chat in Indian Language	S	Fn
	UC 7.	Draft a letter	F	Fn
	UC 8.	Indian Language Calendar	S	Fn, L, V, IP
	UC 9.	Indian Almanac	S	Fn, L, V, IP
		(DT)		

F.   Examples of UDL and ADL

F1.1 *User Domain Lexicon (UDL)*

Table F1. Sample of User Domain Lexicon (UDL)

No.	Words/ Phrases	Languag e/ Script	Definition	Context of application	Mental Models
Task 1. Data entry of museum records					
Nouns					
1.1	Record	English / English	Information of an artifact based on fixed set of parameters like title, historical background, age, etc.	The record of an artifact is referred for more information.	
1.3	Accesion No.	English / English	A unique number by which a record can be retrieved.	While searching the record.	**All museum authorities:** Once assigned an accession no. to an artifact, nobody can change it. There is no standard numbering discipline. We can guess from the style of numbering, in whose tenure an artifact was inducted.
Verbs					
1.4	Classify	English / English	All objects in a museum are classified based on theme, period, materials.	Classification is helpful in searching a particular artifact.	**Curator:** An object can be classified under many categories. Categories are infinite in number. Not all are known. There can be difference of views to a classification.
1.5	Comment	English / English	Suggestions for improving the quality of a record.	Director and Curator write their comments and return the draft of a record to curator.	**Data Entry Operator:** Curator's comments are about typographic errors. Director asks for change in content. It takes longer time, as Curator has to rewrite.
1.6	Approve	English / English	The draft of a record is accepted for inclusion in Main Accession Register.	On feeling satisfied with the contents of a record, Director approves it.	**Data Entry Operator & Curator:** Once approved no more changes can be made. Sr. Curator can also approve if the Director delegates his power. Curator cannot approve a record.
1.7	De-access	English / English	Certain entries are temporarily removed from register.	While giving some objects on loan. But these entries are restored after loan period is over.	
Adjectives					
1.8	Sensitive	English / English	A record as a subject of dispute	For keeping some information confidential.	**All:** Most people avoid working on a disputed topic.
Phrases					
1.9	Main Accession Register	English / English	A notebook in which all records are properly indexed and documented	To find final records	
1.10	Conservation report	English / English	Documentation of damages introduced in an artifact	Useful in identifying damages introduced over a period.	

F1.2 Application Domain Lexicon (ADL)

Table F2. Sample of Application Domain Lexicon (ADL)

No.	Words/ Phrases	Language / Script	Definition	Context of application	Mental Models
Task 1. Data entry of museum records					
Nouns					
1.1	Homepage	English / English	The first page of the application accessible from anywhere within the application. The central location where the root links for navigation are available.	The place from where one enters the virtual museum.	--
1.2	Module	English / English	A unit for defining a part of something.	The location where all approved records are visible. The location where the subscription details are found.	A group or a distinct set of related activities clubbed together in software.
Verbs					
1.3	Update	English / English	Incorporate the latest information.	Improving the quality of information in a record by adding latest information.	Saving any type of modification.
1.4	Submit	English / English	To allow oneself to be subjected to something imposed or to be undergone.	Saving the newly created record and sending a copy of it to curator for checking.	Adding the information to the database.
1.5	Delete	English / English	Completely remove or erase the existence of something.	Removal of record from Main Accession Register (As per the museum rules deletion is not permitted).	The record is deleted from Main Accession Register but in the background it is actually moved to some other location. It is never deleted.
Phrases					
1.7	Display Page	English / English	Presenting the required information on computer screen.	Previewing the final record.	--
1.7	Display All Entries	English / English	Presenting the links of required information on computer screen.	Showing the list of records.	
1.8	Display Files	English / English /	Presenting the list of data files on computer screen.	Showing the attached multimedia objects like video clips, images, 3D models.	--

F1.3 Examples of Linguistic Metaphors

Following definitions and examples of linguistic ontological metaphors are from the book named 'Metaphors We Live By' [Lakoff et al., 1980].

1. Entity and Substance Metaphors

Ontological metaphor offers experience of physical objects providing substance and orientational references to abstract concepts.

Examples:

- Inflation is *rising*. (Entity)
- We are *working towards* peace. (Referring)
- It will take *a lot of patience* to finish this job. (Quantifying)
- *The pressure* of responsibilities.

2. Personification

Inputting the human qualities to things that are not human.

- *Life* has cheated me.
- *Cancer* finally caught up with him.
- Our biggest *enemy* is inflation.

2. Orientational Metaphors

Using spatial or directional references with concepts which are not physical in nature.

- It requires *deeper* understanding.
- *High* status is up, *low* status is down.
- All *up coming* events are enlisted.
- His mood is *low*.

4. Metonymy

Using one entity to refer another that is related to it.

- *Food* is waiting for you.
- *Acrylic* has taken over the art world.

G. Examples of Heuristic Criteria

G1. Familiarity

G1.1 Existing Knowledge

Example 1.

During the project of 3D Watershed Game for villagers, the progress of time was to be indicated as part of the user interface. The period of four years is miniaturized to one-hour duration in the game. During brainstorming sessions, ideas like 'calendar' and 'clock' were suggested for this purpose. Both ideas got rejected as they belong to 'day-to-day knowledge dimension' of educated people. Figure G1. shows scheduler metaphor that uses both 'calendar' and 'clock' representations.

Figure G1. Scheduler Icon in AVG Anti Virus Utility

The 'calendar' metaphor was ruled out, as it is unfamiliar to illiterate villagers. It was observed that the villagers display the calendar in their houses only for its decorative value. Both ideas involved reading of text. Considering this background, it was decided to represent time by designing a season indicator. It contained the pictures of Summer, Rainy and Winter seasons. The sub-segments (indication of months) under the block of every season were highlighted for showing the progress of time.

Figure G2. Pictorial representations of various seasons

Example 2.

Photo album, artist's portfolio and catalog were considered as alternative *candidate interface metaphors* during the development of QuickMM Album Author. The software is targeted to photographers and event managers. Its applications are meant for general masses. At the prima-facie assessment, one realizes that proposed user group is likely to depend upon 'day-to-day knowledge dimension'.

In this case, the *candidate interface metaphors* have following knowledge dimensions-

Photo Album: Day-to-day

Portfolio: Professional / Educational

Catalog: Professional / Educational

Cataloging requires knowledge of standards and indexing techniques. Librarians and archiving experts are trained with cataloging skills. Whereas, artists, architects and investors use portfolios for managing large documents. 'Photo album' is the most familiar metaphor for the specified users as it belongs to day-to-day knowledge dimension.

It was decided to chose 'photo album' as interface metaphor to start with and consider the 'portfolio' and 'catalog' as supporting metaphors, which could be useful during the advanced versions of this software.

G1.2 Generality

Example 3.

The use of 'classroom as interface metaphor in Inscript Typing Tutor meets the generality criteria as it is most common to all students. It also properly encompasses the clusters of functionalities in the software.

Figure G3. World Start and Stop Icons in Cult 3D

Example 4.

Figure G3. shows the 'world start' and 'stop' icons represented as traffic signals in Cult 3D software. These icons perfectly meet the generality criteria as most users are exposed to traffic signals.

G2. Similarity

G2.1 Structure

Refer the example of coherent and diverse interface metaphors given in Chapter 5. for structural similarity.

G2.2 Behavior

Example 5.

There cannot be many functional similarities between the software and interface metaphor. For example, the internal mechanism of a brush tool in Adobe Photoshop is altogether different than the real brush. But both serve the same purpose. Functional characteristics of the brush in terms of its size, stroke thickness and quality, and the ink flow are designed to behave similar to the real brush.

Example 6.

As shown in Figure G13. NVIDIA QuadroView uses round buttons for rotating the 3D model in X,Y and Z axis. The functional characteristics of round buttons provided in software are exactly similar to the buttons used in devices like Radio, Tape Recorder, etc. The Photoshop software provides a toolbox. It has inherited many affordances of a real toolbox. It contains various tools and can be moved around the screen as required.

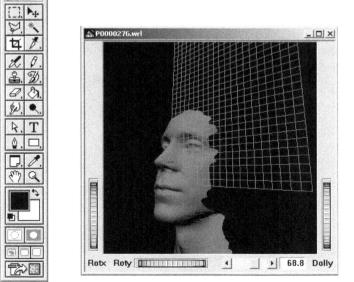

Figure G4. Round buttons in NVIDIA QuadroView and Toolbox of Photoshop

Example 7.

Figure G5. Shelves in Maya Software

As shown in Figure G5. Maya software has used the concept of shelves in which various tools can be stacked and removed if not required. The magical aspect of these shelves is that they are scrollable. The affordances of a real shelf are perfectly captured in the form of functionality.

G2.3. Spatial Layout

Example 8.

The Divex DVD player shown in Figure G6. emulates Television and VCR through its spatial layout. Presto Mr. Photo software shown in Figure G12. is also an excellent example of spatial layout.

Figure G6. Television and VCR metaphor used in Divex Player

Example 9.

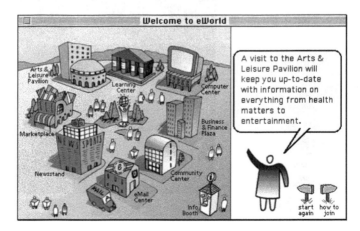

Figure G7. Village metaphor used by Apple e-World Online Service

Figure G7. shows how the 'village' interface metaphor was used by Apple e-world wherein every feature is represented as landmark buildings or towers. Each building is actually a hyperlink.

Example 10.

Figure G8. shows how the 'temple' metaphor is used for presenting the index of chapters and other philosophical scriptures. It provides a conceptual model for the users to easily recall the location of every link in the index. The temple metaphor is illustrated by saint *Dnyaneshwar* through lyrical verses in the 18th chapter of *Dnyaneshwari*. A 3D model of temple metaphor is constructed in VRML format for giving hyperlinks to various chapters in three-dimensional space. This helped us in adding spatial cues to the conceptual structure [Katre, 2002]. In this case, we found that the conceptual structure of interface metaphor is serving like a mnemonic in recalling the order and names of chapters and philosophical scriptures.

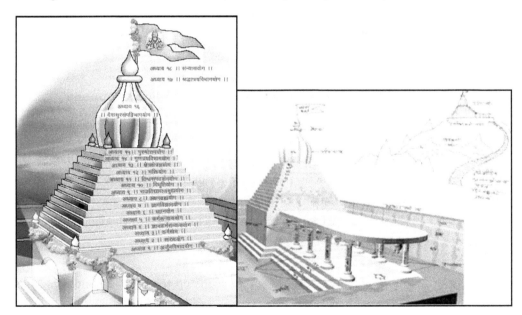

Figure G8. Temple metaphor in *Dnyaneshwari*

Example 11.

During the digital library project, the author of this dissertation asked a librarian to recall and describe the path for reaching the location where the volumes of Encyclopedia Britannica are kept in the library. The librarian used references of architectural elements, colors, shapes and spatial directions during the narration of the path. He also performed mental rotations of 3D space, defined relative positions of objects in his mind, until reaching the specific location on the bookshelf where the encyclopedia was kept. This experiment proves the fact that spatial clues are extremely important for good memory recall [Katre, 2004a].

G3. Extensibility

G3.1 Relevance and Longevity
Example 12.

Figure G9. Mobile phones with icons of 'land-line telephone'

The modern mobile handsets have the 'land-line telephone' as an icon on their keypads. This is because the present generation of consumers is initially exposed to land-line telephones. It is part of their existing knowledge and mental model. The new generations, which are directly exposed to mobile phones, may not require this type of icon. Therefore the longevity of this interface metaphor is maximum 10 years in developing countries. In fact some mobile handsets used in developed countries already do not have this icon.

The better option is to use 'mouth' and 'ear' as icons on the mobile handsets. These icons will never lose relevance.

G4. Compatibility

G4.1.Customizability
Example 13.

The *Ganesh* (the *Hindu* god symbolizing the source of universal intellect and knowledge) metaphor from *Dnyaneshwari* includes several metaphoric concepts that are customized to meet the requirement of communication. The *Puranas* (Indian mythological scriptures) are written in total eighteen parts. Therefore, saint *Dnyaneshwar* visualized lord Ganesh wearing a necklace with eighteen beads as the representation of eighteen *Puranas* as shown in Figure G10.

Normally, lord Ganesh has four hands as per the Indian mythology. But because *Dnyaneshwar* wanted to represent *Shadadarshanas* (six different disciplines of Indian philosophy), he visualized lord *Ganesh* with six hands.

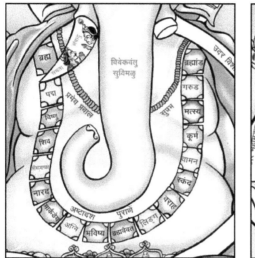 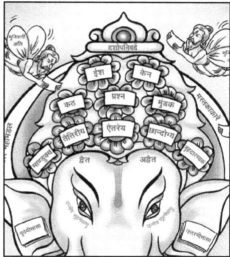

Figure G10. Eighteen *Puranas* as beads of necklace and crown with ten flowers as *Upanishadas* of lord *Ganesh*

Also because there are ten *Unpanishadas* (Indian philosophical scripture), saint *Dnyaneshwar* visualizes the crown of lord *Ganesh* decorated with ten flowers representing the ten *Unpanishadas* as shown in Figure G10. In this example, the number of beads in the necklace, the number of hands of lord Ganesh and the number of flowers on the crown are adjusted or customized to meet the requirement of the application.

G5. *Representability*

G5.1. Appearance
Example 14.

The appearance of bookshelf, books and reading stand in Keebook Creator software as shown in Figure C1. is very distinct and easy to recognize. The software supports giving unique colors to book jackets for quick identification. The sizes of books, shelf, and reading stand are closer to real.

In Figure C2. the slate is of the same size as the blackboard. It should have been slightly smaller in size.

Example 15.

In some situations, the reference object selected as interface metaphor has an ambiguous form, e.g., the concept of 'paperweight' is introduced in Inscript Typing Tutor. The software has a feature for temporarily saving the drawing. The user has to just drag the 'paperweight' on to the drawing area for this purpose.

Several options for depicting this metaphor were explored but most subjects failed to recognize the graphical representation of the paperweight. The reason of its failure is the ambiguous appearance of paperweight itself. It lacks distinct and recognizable form. There are paperweights of varied types like metal statues, glass balls, dolls and other unconventional forms.

Example 16.

Figure G11. Light box metaphor of PhotoDisc

The 'light box' metaphor introduced for selection of images in PhotoDisc software, is a good idea. The designers and artists are familiar with the 'lightbox' concept and its application. But if you see the presentation of so-called 'light box' metaphor in Figure G11., it hardly conveys anything to do with it. The interface metaphor is presented only at textual level. It completely lacks visual appearance.

Example 17.

Figure G12. Lightbox in Presto Mr. Photo Software

Contrary to the earlier example, the depiction of 'light box' metaphor in Presto Mr. Photo software shown in Figure G12. is closer to real.

G5.2. Depiction
Example 18.

The depiction of 'classroom' metaphor in Typing Tutor software as shown in Figure C2. is very realistic as the schoolchildren are less likely to comprehend abstract or subtle depiction of interface metaphor.

Example 19.

Figure G13. Gesture Icon in DataGlove Manager, e-mail video and clear video icons in Presto VideoWorks software

At times, the realistic portrayal of metaphor is perceived as literal depiction of metaphor. But it is necessary for certain type of users. The gesture icon shown in Figure G13. is a typical example of bad depiction and semantics. It does not convey anything about gestures. As per the lexical analysis of the icon, the lens is completely unnecessary. Also the 'e-mail video' and 'clear video' icons do not portray the idea properly.

Whether the depiction has to be very realistic, optimized or stylized depends on the visual literacy of users. The season indicator shown in Figure G2. is designed with more realism. It provides maximum number of visual clues to make it understandable to villagers. On the contrary, Figure G14. shows an abstract and oversimplified graphic forms that were found extremely difficult for the villagers to understand.

Figure G14. Oversimplified form of season indicator

G6. Cognitive Ergonomics

G6.1 Mental Model
Example 20.

The 'In/Out trays' and 'register' are used as interface metaphors in JATAN: Virtual Museum Builder. Commentary of Task Performance (CTP) shows that these objects are part of the regular workflow of museums. Naturally, these are part of the mental model of the museum staff. These interface metaphors exactly represent certain functionalities of the software.

G6.2 Semantics
Example 21.

The 'season indicator' proposed in the 3D Game is workable only in *Maharashtra* state of India. The distribution of seasons in other geographic regions is likely to be different. Therefore, the semantic properties of season indicator are true and consistent only for the users from *Maharashtra* state. This defines the limitations of semantic suitability of the 'season indicator' metaphor.

Figure G15. Key-frame icons used in Maya uoftware

Example 22.

Key-frames used in animation have nothing to do with the actual 'key' object as shown in Figure G15. In animation, key frame means, the frame that marks the distinct position in a motion. In this example, the semantic properties of 'key' attributed to 'key frame' are false and hence misleading. Semantically, it is an imprecise representation. The novice users are likely to take it in literal sense.

Example 23.

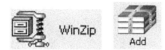

Figure G16. File compression icons of WinZip and WinRAR

Semantically, the Winzip icon, which shows the jack being used for compressing the collection of files, is more correct and obvious. It is also consistent with the desktop metaphor of Windows. Whereas, the WinRAR, another application of similar type, uses an icon showing a set of books tied together using a belt. It lacks generality when it comes to representing the files. One is likely to misinterpret it for book archival only. Refer example 18. for wrong semantics.

G6.3 Syntactic

Example 24.

In Figure G3. the 'world' concept is not represented in the icon. In the same figure, the third icon is titled as 'world step'. Ideally, all three icons should have the 'world' as a common lexical element. It is reflected in textual propositions. All three icons, if viewed together lack the syntactic quality.

Example 25.

Figure G17. Syntactic Design of Icons from Maya

Figure G17. shows a series of icons that convey various functionalities relating with surface modeling such as trim surface, cancel trimming, attach surface, cut surface, extend surface, edit surface, etc. It reveals the pattern of logic through the design of icons. But these are a set of icons only. It is desired that the entire conceptual structure, layouts, icons, text, sounds, dialogs, and functionality all to be woven syntactically. Such examples are rare to find.

Example 26.

In 'classroom' metaphor, as soon as the children recognized the slate, all other concepts like toolbox, schoolbag, books, etc. got recognized. Figure C2. shows how the background layout can contribute to the syntactic design of interface metaphor.

G6.4 Comprehensibility

Example 27.

Many times the referred object is recognized by the users but they fail to understand the associated proposition.

Figure G18. Headlight Icon in NVIDIA QuadroView

The NVIDIA QuadroView software uses the 'table lamp' icon for representing the 'headlight' feature. While navigating through the 3D environment it is required to switch on the headlight for visibility in 3D space. This is an obvious case where the 'referred' and 'referent' are not matching. The associated proposition (referent) is titled as 'headlight'. But the icon (referred) shows a table lamp. It can also be an example of wrong semantics.

G7. Feasibility

G7.1 GUI Constraints

Example 28.

**Figure G19. Slider visualized (A) and the actual
implementation (B) for Typing Tutor software**

Figure G19. shows how the slider for reducing and increasing the speed of animation was visualized (A) and what was actually implemented in the software (B). It indicates the slight compromises made on the look and feel of the slider due to the constraints of GUI implementation. But still the final result is quite closer to original multimedia visualization.

Example 29.

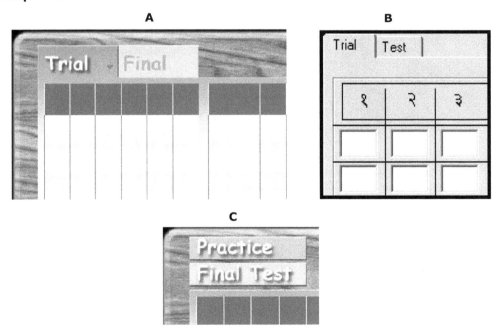

Figure G20. Visualization of tabs

In the same software, tabs are used for switching between the trial and test of every typing lesson. Based on the visualization and multimedia rendering, the software developer immediately foresaw the constraints of changing the visual appearance of tabs in Visual Basic. This feedback helped in exploring other feasible alternatives. Finally option C was selected in place of tabs as shown in Figure G22.

H.   Multimedia Rendering of Interface Metaphor

Figure H1. shows how the traversal of a museum record between the In and Out trays of data entry operator, curator and director is visualized using multimedia. In this example three consoles of the members participating in the transaction are visualized in the same sequence. This interface metaphor is rendered using interactive multimedia for JATAN: Virtual Museum Builder.

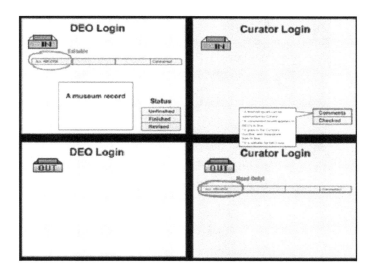

Figure H1. Traversal of a record through
In/Out trays rendered using multimedia

I.   Sample of Captured Mental Models

As shown in Table A1 in Appendix A, around 7 subjects participated in the usability acceptance test of certain interface components designed for the 3D Watershed Game Project. The author of this dissertation conceptualized and designed the interface metaphors and also conducted the usability tests on 4th Oct. 2004 to find whether the mental model is properly captured or not. The results of the test are given below whish eloquent enough.

Figure I1. Usability Testing

Figure I2. Season Indicator

Test 1.: Visual Depiction

Interface Component 1.: Season Indicator To Show Progress of Time

> **Test Results:**
>
> Immediately recognized: 4
>
> Recognized after some prompting: 3
>
> Subject No. 2 required long time for recognition due to poor eyesight. He admitted that he had eyesight problem. Many of them used a term called *Pankalaa* for rainy season.
>
> **Acceptance:**
>
> All subjects accepted the representation of seasons.
>
> **Suggestions:**

Some of them felt that the depiction of rain showers and clouds should be more accentuated.

Conclusion:

The details mentioned above may be accentuated further. With a bit of introduction the season indicator will be immediately understandable to almost all villagers. The season indicator is unanimously accepted.

Test 2.: Representation of Months in Season Indicator

Test Results:

Immediately recognized: 3

Recognized after some prompting: 3

- The subject with poor eyesight had a problem in figuring out the visuals.
- 2 subjects were confused by the color of animated progress bar.

Acceptance:

All subjects accepted the representation of months as 12 different slots (4 slots per season).

Suggestions:

There was no concrete suggestion.

Conclusion:

'Month' being an abstract concept does not have the concrete visual form. The subjects after a bit of introduction were able to calculate the months. The depiction of months is unanimously accepted.

Figure I3. Sliding cupboards as user interface

Test 3.:

Interface Component 2: Sliding Cupboards with Tabs as Tool Containers

The test also involved usage of touch screen interface. After touching the handle, the cupboard slides into the screen. It contains objects like spade, sickle, axe, gas cylinder. There are several cupboards with different sets of tools in them.

Test Results:

Immediately recognized: 7

- 2/3 subjects kept on pressing their finger on the touch screen. They were not releasing it immediately.
- Some of them did not click in the centre of the button and hence no effect was visible.
- After practicing it 3 / 4 times everyone could do it properly.
- Subjects used words like *Mandani* and *Kapaat* for cupboard in their local dialect.

Acceptance:

All subjects accepted the representations.

Suggestions:

There was no concrete suggestion.

Conclusion:

Overall refinement of visuals in terms of visual clarity. The shape of cupboard should be optimized. The cupboard with tools representation is unanimously accepted.

The 'cupboard' metaphor used in this case, is also a good example of 'customizability' heuristic discussed in Chapter 9. It will be possible to explore different variations of the same metaphor. It will allow us to add or reduce the number of shelves in them or reduce the sizes of cupboards. It also has certain magical super-affordances like tabs as handles and the slide in/out feature.

J.   Remote Usability Testing

Research paper on remote usability testing is presented from next page onwards.
The experience of remote usability testing using UniFace was presented during a seminar on User Centred Design (UCD) organized by Indo European Usability Systems Partnership (IESUP) and Computer Society of India at Mumbai during Oct. 2003.

A research paper on this subject was also presented during Easy 2004 conference. The citation is given below.

Katre D (2004). Experimenting with UniFace: A Tool for Usability Testing of Icons, ACM-SIGCHI-SI National Usability Conference Easy 2004, Bangalore, India.

Aaron Marcus who is on the editorial board of ACM Interactions was present during Easy 2004 conference at Bangalore to deliver his keynote address. He generously appreciated the presentation on above paper.

UniFace: Internet based Software for Remote Usability Testing of Icons

Dinesh S. Katre
Centre for Development of Advanced Computing (C-DAC)
Ministry of Communications and Information Technology, Government of India,
Agriculture College Campus, Near District Industries Centre,
Shivaji Nagar, Pune 411005, India.
Tel/Fax: 91+020+5533250
dinesh@cdacindia.com

ABSTRACT

The Graphical User Interface (GUI) of software usually consists of huge number of icons. Though the intention is to improve the usability of software, not all interface designers are able to test and evaluate the comprehensibility of icons. Increasing exposure to unevaluated icons causes cognitive fatigue to users and slows down the intuitive learning. Users from diverse geographic locations, cultures and religions are very likely to interpret and understand these icons differently. As software products are designed to address universal needs, testing and evaluation of GUI across the globe or at least, wherever the product is likely to be used becomes important. Creation of dedicated usability labs in various locations for usability testing is not a viable proposition. A software tool named '*UniFace*' for remote usability testing of icons is designed capitalizing on far-reaching capability of Internet. *UniFace* extends the usability lab onto the desktop of every user. It encourages stakeholder participation in the design process and captures their perceptions. The testing methods of *UniFace* produce various reports with measurable and eloquent data for empirical analysis. The database of icon properties and test results can be helpful in visualizing the cognitive models of various user groups. *UniFace* has the potential to facilitate the standardization of iconic language for GUI design. It can prove very useful for offshore software projects.

Keywords

GUI, Icons, Remote Usability Testing, Cognitive Model, Measurable Data, Stakeholder Participation

FLOOD OF ICONS

The sign language of icons is becoming complex day-by-day due to increasing number of icons introduced through operating systems, software packages and websites. Its vocabulary is ever evolving and multiplying very rapidly. Our observations reveal that a novice computer user needs familiarity with minimum 40 to 50 icons on Windows platform for basic word processing using MS Word. An average computer professional has familiarity with at least 300 to 400 icons. When counted the number of icons on a computer of a multimedia professional, it crossed the thousand mark. The users get exposed to more and more icons as they navigate through various software products. Young computer users can take extra efforts for learning new icons and memorize many of them but the older people show significant decline in their ability to recall [13]. Resultantly, the training needs have grown out of shape, as many novice users need to learn the definitions of icons. Organizations have to spend a lot of money since users take paid time to get trained [28]. This proves the fact that not all iconic interfaces are comprehensible and usable as expected.

Need of Measuring the Usability of Icons

Most designers tend to test the comprehensibility of icons on their teammates or on a few subjects or simply ignore testing by documenting the definitions of icons as part of online help. The excessive and unevaluated usage of such icons must be causing significant cognitive stress, irritation and prolonged learning for software users. The testing reveals that several icons are actually misleading, ambiguous, conflicting and unnecessary [25, 15, 11]. In the past, there have been major research explorations for identifying the guidelines of interface designing [7]. On the basis of these guidelines, most interface designers build their hypothesis of how users would interpret the icons. But how effectively the designer has succeeded in transferring the theoretical guidelines into design [30] needs to be measured and evaluated based on factual data [21].

Constraining Factors of Usability Testing

The sign language of icons has to be universalized [19] for precise communication especially when software products are addressing universal applications and utilities. Intercultural issues referring to the religious, historical, linguistic, aesthetic, and other more humanistic issues of particular groups or peoples, sometimes crossing national boundaries need to be addressed for achieving greater acceptability to the products [20]. The generality and adaptability [2] of iconic interfaces can be achieved through externalization of our thoughts, ideas and concepts [8] for inviting criticism and user participation in the design process [11]. But the prohibitive factor is the cost of setting up usability labs for testing of iconic interfaces in geographically distributed locations [27]. Involving usability experts and renting the facilities for such testing makes it an unrealistic proposition. All such impeding factors highlight the importance of "discount usability engineering" approach [22]. In this situation, the only option is to explore remote usability testing methods [23].

In summary, the observations and requirements of usability testing narrated above necessitate the development of remote usability testing methods and a far-reaching mechanism for encouraging participation of users from diverse geographic locations.

Difficulties of Interface Design Students & Instructors

C-DAC's National Multimedia Resource Centre, Pune, India conducts training programs to teach multimedia. The students are introduced to various interface design issues with special emphasis on interactive multimedia software. In an exclusive academic project, the students are asked to design icons representing various links and functions of software. Every year, around 84 students produce approx. 1500 icons for varied themes of software. Evaluation of these icons is extremely challenging and a mammoth task. Awarding higher grades to icons, which are very easily understandable but not very well rendered, often invites disagreement of students. Many times beautifully rendered icons, yet based on ambiguous metaphors [5] do not communicate well. The instructor grades the projects based on his/her personal understanding of icons. The difference of viewpoints between the students and the instructor

results into disputes at the time of grading. This is due to unavailability of definite testing methods and inability to measure / quantify the usability of huge number of icons designed by students.

The frequent disagreements with students about grading of their iconic interfaces forced us to devise a mechanism that could enable them in exploring third party evaluation themselves. The outcome of this experiment is found beneficial to not only the students but also the usability experts.

By and large these are common problems faced by most interface designers and usability experts. Testing methods like open-ended written comprehension, multiple choices have been already proposed and experimented for finding out the plausible response to a set of symbols [10, 25, 3, 6, 31]. As documented in Wolff's ANSI report, a large hall with proper seating arrangement, printed booklet with the symbols for testing and two judges were required for conducting the tests. Major amount of time was invested for collating the feedback of subjects. The Internet based solution described in this paper incorporates existing as well new methods for confirming the results.

UNIFACE: AN INTERNET BASED METHOD FOR USABILITY TESTING & EVALUATION OF ICONS

UniFace offers very simple, clear and result oriented Internet based usability testing methods. Eloquence of data captured by *UniFace* reduces the dependency on usability experts [16]. Following are the prominent features / characteristics of *UniFace*-

- Tests the comprehensibility / usability of icons within the design phase.
- Allows conducting of remote usability tests in diverse geographic locations for wider user participation in design process.
- Captures and maintains the record of user profiles and test results.
- Stores the database of icons with variety of attributes.
- Helps interface designers in visualizing the cognitive models of defined user groups.
- Produces measurable statistics and usable reports for substantiating the decisions [21].
- Provides a simplified procedural template for usability testing of icons that can be used by small-scale software developers.

No.	Names of Modules	Performed by	Activities
I	Integration	Interface Designer	To integrate the icons along with their properties
II	Testing	Targeted Users (Subjects)	To record the feedback
III	Evaluation	Usability Expert	To observe, interpret and judge the feedback of subjects

Table 1. Basic Modules of *UniFace*

Introduction to the basic modules of *UniFace*

UniFace is developed using web technologies and has three modules namely, Integration, Testing and Evaluation as shown in Table 1. Access to users and designers is controllable project as well as module wise.

Some aspects relating to 'Attributes of Icons' mentioned in this paper are based on information already reported in journals. This information is briefly given in the paper so as to fully communicate the testing methods and the design of *UniFace*.

Module I- Integration of Icons

Having designed the icons, the designer has to start with the Integration Module of *UniFace*. One begins by creating a separate project with appropriate name. A project can include various segments / subsets of icons. Each segment can be named appropriately as e.g. toolbar, editor, etc. Figure 1. illustrates the overall structure of Integration Module.

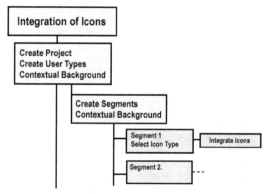

Figure 1. Design of Integration Module

Every icon has certain inherent attributes such as rendering style, type, form, associated proposition, title and visual elements. The interface designer has to indicate the attributes of an icon by selecting appropriate options at the time of integration. *UniFace* maintains a record of these attributes in the database. The definitions of the basic attributes of icons are elaborated hereafter.

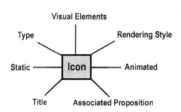

Figure 2. Attributes of an Icon

The designer has to indicate the pictorial quality of icons in terms of 'optimized' and 'moderate' rendering styles [16]. Brief explanation of these rendering styles is given below-

Optimized Rendering

Many icons used in software packages such as MS Office are rendered in optimized manner. The icons are pretty small in size (16 x 16 or 32 x 32 pixels). These icons are oversimplified and have just minimum necessary details.

Moderate Rendering

If compared with optimally rendered icons, moderately rendered icons are quite detailed and colorful. The icon size is much larger (64 x 64 pixels and above).

Rendering styles have to be indicated, as the recognition of optimized icons is at times slower than that of moderately rendered icons. Chances of a person recognizing the moderately rendered icon are higher. Also, the rendering style has an implication on recall value of an icon. In addition, the designer has to select whether the icons belong to object, action and concept types [29]. Following are the definitions and critical aspects relating to each type of icon.

Object Icons

As these icons represent real life objects they are very easy to illustrate and recognize. The weakness of these icons is lack of proportional details, which at times leads to misinterpretation by user.

Figure 3. Object Icons

Action Icons

'Action Icons' are very difficult to illustrate and understand as depiction of an action or a process involves two or more stages. The designer often uses arrows while depicting the element of time or before and after stages in action icons. Action icons can be best communicated in the form of an animation.

Figure 4. Action Icons

Concept Icons

The designer tries to build analogies by showing some arbitrary [25] or metaphoric images while representing abstract features of software. Users from different cultures are very likely to misinterpret the concept icons.

Figure 5. Concept Icons

Form

Animated icons are found very effective in places where static icons fail to deliver the message. The software products have both forms of icons (static and animated) used as part of the GUI.

Associated Proposition and Title

Associated proposition means the intended message to be communicated by an icon. This message is then compressed in one or two words as the title of an icon. Users usually remember the icon with its title if both are resonating the same meaning.

Visual Elements of an Icon

Visual elements used in icons such as computer, arrow, brush, globe and chain, tick mark, etc. also have to be mentioned as part of icon attributes in *UniFace*. We come across varied permutations and combinations of these visual elements composed for communicating different shades of messages.

For the first time, *UniFace* has integrated and woven all attributes of icons together as important parameters of usability testing and analysis.

Define Stratified User Groups

Having integrated all icons as mentioned earlier, the interface designer has to now define the targeted user categories. These are broad categories of users such as tourists, accountants, medical practitioners, teachers, students, etc. It is expected that users representing all such categories be tested through *UniFace*. If a particular category of users is not tested then the report produced by *UniFace* indicates the same.

UniFace supports creation of user accounts under every stratified group by entering their basic information like name, company, e-mail address, etc. Projects already integrated in *UniFace* can be allotted to users for which they comply the eligibility criteria. Unique User IDs and passwords get e-mailed to users along with a list of projects.

Contextual Background

The designer has to provide a small write-up about the software product in *UniFace*, as recognition and interpretation of icons is quite context dependent. In addition, it is possible to link the screenshot of overall interface layout showing other related icons. The subjects can read the write-up and view the screenshot of interface layout before starting the test.

Integration of Multiple Clues

At this stage, the designer is supposed to input total three clues for every icon. It consists of one clue expressing the desired proposition and the other two clues communicating the probable and yet misleading propositions. Having completed this preparatory work, *UniFace* gets ready for performing various tests.

The batch of Sept. 2002 to March 2003 of Diploma in Advanced Computer Arts course tested around 13 GUI projects using *UniFace* at C-DAC, Pune, India. The students accessed *UniFace* on Intranet and were permitted to perform the tests on minimum 6 subjects per project due to time constraints. Overall around 74 subjects participated in the tests. Broad characteristics of test results are derived based on observations recorded during the experiments.

MODULE II- TESTING

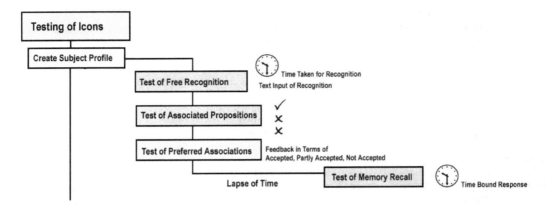

Figure 6. Design of Testing Module

Objectives of Testing

Interface designers and usability experts must be very clear about the objectives of testing. Various tests as indicated in Figure 6. are performed to find out whether the icons are-

- easy to interpret and understand.
- communicating precise message.
- easy to memorize and recall.
- ambiguous and confusing.
- are slow communicators.
- needing initial introduction.

Above objectives largely determine whether the icons pass or fail the test. One can capitalize on the feedback captured by *UniFace* for meeting the following objectives-

- Observe the trends and unique characteristics of response received from various user groups and improvise the icons.
- Try to visualize the mental model of subjects on the basis of data captured by *UniFace*.
- In case of favorable results, certify the icons for integration in the software.

Precautions

The tests performed using *UniFace* can produce best results if certain precautions are taken. They are as under-

- Send an e-mail communication mentioning the User ID and URL for accessing *UniFace* and guidelines of the test to various user groups. Ensure that the subject profiles are properly matching with the groups defined earlier.

- Inform the subjects that the intention is not to examine their abilities but to get their feedback for improvising the GUI.
- The subjects must go through the test alone and not in a group. They should refrain from showing the testing process to others. If their colleagues or friends are interested in participating in the testing process then they must do it individually.
- The subject should be requested to fill their profiles sincerely and completely.
- While performing the test they should avoid other interruptions and complete the test without spending time anywhere else.

Create Subject Profile

It is mandatory for the subject to enter his profile details in the beginning of the testing module. Figure 7. shows the template for entering the subject profiles. It requires information on items such as Name, Age, Gender, Computer Awareness, Academic, Economic, Cultural / Ethnic background, Geographic Location and User Group. This information gets stored in the database of *UniFace*.

After completely filling the required profile details, the Subject is then allowed to begin with the first 'Test of Free Recognition'.

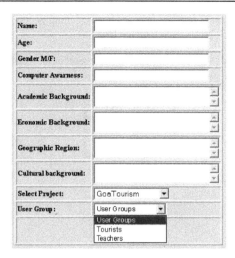

Figure 7. Template for Preparing Subject Profile

Test of Free Recognition (TFR)

In this particular test, only one icon is displayed on computer screen at a time without mentioning its title or associated proposition or clues as shown in Figure 8. The subject can wait until he has understood the icon and then type his response in the input area. In case of failing to recognize the icon, the subject can mention the same and move on to next icon. *UniFace* calculates and records the time taken for recognition starting from the display of icon up to clicking on 'next icon' link in the input area. The subject can refer the contextual information if needed.

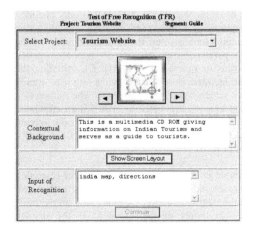

Figure 8. Test of Free Recognition (TFR)

The TFR generates feedback about whether the visual elements rendered in the icon are recognizable and the visual semantics is conveying the associated proposition. The interface designer immediately comes to know whether the keywords are closer to the intended message of the icon or else. If the icons are designed with semiotic qualities then the rate of recognition is higher and faster as the test progresses. If the first icon is understood then the forthcoming icons are also grasped quickly but inconsistent and conflicting representations cause confusion [29].

The response generated by TFR can be characterized as under-

- The record of time indicates that ambiguous icons require longer time for recognition.
- The subject-
  - fails to understand an icon even after taking long time.
  - ends up describing the visual elements depicted in an icon but fails to capture the associated proposition.
  - associates an icon with some other function of software or misinterprets.
  - correctly associates an icon with the desired function or utility of software in short time.

Ambiguous icons indicate a common trend of long time taken for recognition. Subjects attempt blind guesses as well. The recognition input apparently includes a lot of irrelevant information but it is very useful. Subjects are often emotional and very elaborate in their response. You come to know about their vocabulary, proficiency of language and conversance with computer keyboard. Novice computer users make a lot of typographic errors.

The Test of Associated Propositions (TAP) becomes active as soon as the subject is through with TFR.

Test of Associated Propositions (TAP)

TAP displays every icon along with three clues, which are entered by the interface designer during the Integration Module of *UniFace*. The scope of interpretation is reduced to three plausible choices.

Icons help us in building a mental association between the visual and the feature of software. If the association between an icon and the desired proposition is not meaningful then the user is often misled. TAP captures the probability of an icon misleading the subject.

The response generated by TAP can be characterized as under-

- Many times, the icon, which has failed during TFR but is within the proximity of its message, gets recognized during TAP.
- TAP is useful in identifying icons that need initial introduction. If an icon and its associated proposition have semantic connection then after

initial introduction, the users are able to understand it effortlessly.

- Some icons failed during TFR continue to evoke wrong responses.
- The icons that were properly recognized in the TFR are confirmed during TAP.

The user response reveals impreciseness of an icon e.g. Figure 9. shows that an icon of 'binocular' is designed to represent 'site-seeing' for a website on tourism. Many subjects selected 'binocular' as its correct recognition. This reveals that the element of 'site-seeing' is missing in the icon. Here, the icon has succeeded in communicating the referent but failed to communicate the proposition associated with the referent [15].

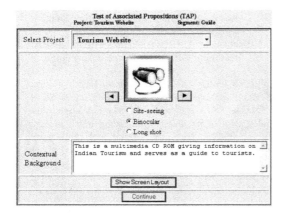

Figure 9. Test of Associated Propositions (TAP)

One may do away with such imprecise icon but what would happen if the standard 'find' feature is required in the website? As the typical 'find' feature is already represented by 'binocular' icon only. You come across many such loosely designed icons in software.

Test of Preferred Associations (TPA)

During this test, an icon along with its associated proposition is displayed on screen. The Subject is requested to give his verdict in terms of whether an icon is accepted, not accepted or partly accepted. The usability expert can corroborate the verdict with the actual response captured during TFR and TAP. TPA produces quantifiable data.

The response generated by TPA can be characterized as under-

- Icons that have failed during TFR and passed during TAP are unanimously accepted.
- Icons that have failed during TFR and TAP unanimously rejected. The subjects very often advise the possible alternatives.

- Subjects suggest improvements / modifications while partly accepting the icon.

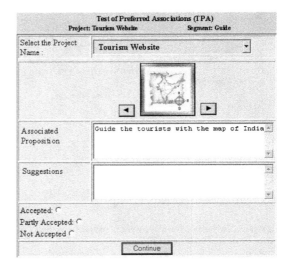

Figure 10. Test of Preferred Associations (TPA)

Test of Memory Recall (TMR)

This test is performed after certain lapse of time to find out whether the subjects are able to recall the icons along with their titles. The lapse duration can be based on frequency of software usage. TMR proves that meaningful association between visual and the title is recalled effortlessly.

So far, in all the tests (TFR, TAP, TPA) only one icon was displayed at a time. TMR displays maximum five icons simultaneously as the cognitive limit of an average person allows tracking of maximum seven items (plus or minus two) [1, 21]. On initiating the test, the identification titles of icons begin to appear on the screen one after another. The subject is expected to click the matching icon within stipulated duration before the next title appears on screen. Having matched all the icons, the subject can go for next lot of icons.

The subject is not given unlimited time for searching or remembering the icon. The usability expert can decide the display duration for every title on the basis of usability goals of GUI design. If the display duration is 5 seconds then the titles randomly change after every 5 seconds.

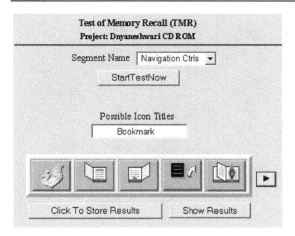

Figure 11. Test of Memory Recall (TMR)

The response generated by TMR can be characterized as under-

- The subject fails to associate the proposition with an ambiguous icon.
- The subject is confused with resembling icons and hence clicks on a wrong icon or fails to make a decision within stipulated time. During the testing of a tourism website, the subjects got confused between the icons of 'water sports' and 'beaches'. This reveals another aspect of impreciseness of an iconic expression.
- Obvious icons are correctly matched with their titles.

TMR can be very useful for testing the recalling ability of older people.

MODULE III- EVALUATION

Module- I

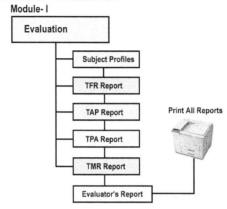

Figure 12. Design of Evaluation Module

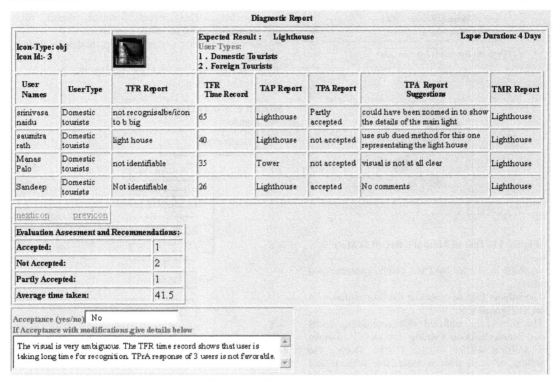

Figure 13. Diagnostic Report

The consolidated diagnostic report as shown in Figure 13. presents overall view of test results pertaining to an icon. The quantifyable aspects of TFR and TPA are presented at the bottom of the report where the usability expert can record his/her decision. Only 4 test results are shown in Figure 13. in order to fit the screenshot in smaller size.

The interface designer has to consider the feedback given by subjects and redesign the faulty icons again. The redesigned icons have to be tested and evaluated through *UniFace* through the same process until there is sufficient acceptance from subjects.

Printouts of all the reports along with the subject profiles are taken and attached to the final diagnostic report. The Interface designer and usability expert have to sign the final report.

A typical evaluation report of a tourism website finalized by the usability expert is shown in Figure 15. In this report, the usability expert has cleared 4 icons without any modification, 7 icons with minor modifications and 3 icons are rejected.

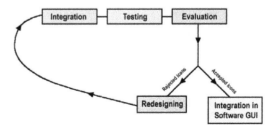

Figure 14. Cycle of Evaluation

IconId	Icon Preview	Title	Modifications	Accepted	Not Accepted	Partly Accepted	Evaluator's Decision
tour-01		Beach	NA	5	1	0	yes
tour-02		Metro Cities	Ambiguity of visual may be reduced.	2	2	2	No
tour-03		Close	The closed door aspect should be more clear. Other decorative details should not standout.	4	1	0	Yes
tour-04		Open	NA	5	0	0	yes
tour-05		Restaurant	NA	4	1	0	yes
tour-06		Forts	More clarity in the visual form.	4	0	1	yes
tour-07		History	may be used with some improvization for depcting scriptures and not for History.	3	2	0	No
tour-08		Map Guide	NA	5	0	0	Yes
tour-09		Museums	Museum aspect should be depicted as this icon may conflict with Harappan Gallery Icon.	4	0	1	Yes
tour-10		Gardens	May be used for conveying greetings.	1	3	1	No
tour-11		Siteseeing	Siteseeing element should be added.	4	0	1	yes
tour-12		Transport	Road transport should also be represented.	5	0	0	Yes

Figure 15. Final Evaluation Report

The cycle of evaluation uncovers certain functions or features that are very difficult to represent in the iconic form. Redesigning and exploration of various visual metaphors do not produce positive results, as not all messages can be communicated effectively using representations [24]. In such cases, the Usability experts may decide not to use any iconic representations and instead use a simple button or a link with its title. This approach can be useful in reducing the pollution of incomprehensible and unnecessary use of icons.

The testing process of *UniFace* reveals the items that should not be shown as icons or the risk associated with it.

Iconographic imagery helps define a larger concept, [4] the symmetry between 'conceptual model' of software and 'interface metaphor'. Indirectly, *UniFace* also collects feedback about the underpinning interface metaphor manifested through icons. If majority of the icons successfully pass through all the tests then the comprehensibility of overall metaphor is also very high.

UniFace is introduced as part of the training programs conducted at C-DAC's National Multimedia Resource Center. The students are able to integrate their interface design projects and test them using *UniFace* on their own. The feedback gathered from the subjects is now agreeable to students without any difference of opinion. The grading of interface design projects is based on empirical analysis. Thus, *UniFace* can completely eliminate the aspect of 'gut feeling' involved in icon designing. One can ensure that icons are really comprehensible enough to the targeted users.

DATABASE OF ICON ATTRIBUTES

Responses captured during TFR and suggestions given in TPA reports can be corroborated with subject profiles for figuring out the mental model of a user group. Of course inputs received during the test may not be adequate for defining the mental model. Usability expert will have to pick up the threads from test results and investigate the subject further.

Table 2. shows how the attributes of icons are stored in the database of *UniFace*. The database is helpful in evolving a lexicon of icons and avoiding overlapping usage of visual elements. There is an icon of Bookmark in Table 2. that shows an open book with a peacock feather as bookmark. This icon is designed for a multimedia CD on *Bhagavadgita* (Hindu religious book). *Bhagavadgita* was first recited by Lord *Krishna* (Hindu God). As per Indian mythology, Lord *Krishna* always has a peacock feather in his crown and therefore we chose to show peacock feather as a bookmark for *Bhagavadgita* CD ROM. This connotation of the icon is specific to Indian culture. This icon need introduction in other regions that India. Thus *UniFace* can capture the problems pertaining to cultural interpretations of icons through its testing process.

Text based search can be performed for identifying the icons that include similar visual elements. Repository of test results and database of icons can be used to find out the following-

- What types of messages are already communicated using similar visual elements?
- Whether the use of proposed visual elements is overlapping with other icons or is it unique enough?
- Do we already have some icon test results of subjects with required profile? This can be a useful input to another project.
- Have those visual elements (icons) positively cleared the tests?
- How recently the tests were performed?
- If subject profiles are suitable then what type of depiction of proposed visual elements they are already familiar with?

The data stored by *UniFace* can be used for prejudging the icons and guiding the efforts of user interface designing in right direction. Variety of testing methods, database of icons with attributes, collection of test results, and accessibility through Internet shows the potential of *UniFace* to facilitate the standardization of iconic language.

CONTINGENCIES AND REMEDIAL OPTIONS

With *UniFace*, it is not possible to monitor the respondents, as they operate from remote locations. In an uncontrollable testing mode, there are chances of a few subjects not performing the tests sincerely. Failing to understand the procedure is also likely if the subjects ignore the guidelines and precautions. But we don't escape these occupational hazards even while testing in a usability lab. For countering such problems, the usability expert can maintain a good dialogue with the subjects through e-mail communication.

Table 2. Properties of icons stored by *UniFace*						
Icon	**Title**	**Associated Proposition**	**Type**	**Rendering Style**	**Form**	**Visual Elements**
	Annotate	Attach annotated comments	Object	Optimized	Static	Paper, Pen
	Status	Indicate status in terms of chapter, pages, verses	Concept	Optimized	Static	Dial, Needles
	Date and Time	Inform the date and time	Concept	Moderate	Static	Calendar, Clock, Dial, Needles
	First Page	Jump to first page	Object	Optimized	Static	Open Book, First Page, Cover
	Help	Open help documents	Concept	Moderate	Static	Closed Book, Question Mark
	MS Word Help	Provide necessary help	Concept	Optimized	Static	Balloon, Question Mark
	Settings and Help	Provide necessary help and controls for settings	Concept	Optimized	Static	Question Mark
	Bookmark	Go to bookmark	Object	Optimized	Static	Open Book, Peacock Feather

Being the stakeholders of proposed software product, the subjects should be convinced about importance of testing and their feedback for positively influencing the design process.

Adequate testing experience of *UniFace* can help the interface designers / usability experts in judging the sincerity of a subject. In case of doubt, one may just entirely disqualify the feedback. Correspondingly, it necessitates that sufficient number of subjects (minimum 20/25 subjects per user group) must be tested.

Even though *UniFace* is far reaching, it is still confined to the parts of world where Internet has spread and sufficient bandwidth is available. Network of cyber-cafes and regional distributors of software products could be involved where the users are unable to access Internet. Involving true stakeholders in the testing process can produce better quality of feedback [9].

At present, only English is supported as part of *UniFace*. Support of regional languages may be required for achieving better communication with subjects from diverse regions.

CONCLUSIONS

UniFace has retained the positive aspects of conventional usability testing methods for evaluation of icons and overcome the constrains such as-

1. Dedicated usability labs are not required. It expands the scope of testing without escalating the cost.
2. It records the time taken by every individual user for TFR.
3. Automates the random shuffling between the titles and icons for TMR.
4. It captures and collates the test results in the form of reports and presents statistical data for analysis.
5. Crosses the geographical boundaries through Internet and allows wider user participation. This can help in revealing the cross-cultural aspects connected with the interpretation of icons.

In addition, *UniFace* provides a reliable testing framework for improving the quality and precision of communication through icons. It offers following advantages.

6. Usability expert can take decisions substantiated by enough evidence and measurable data captured by *UniFace*. The reports generated by *UniFace* clearly indicate which icons have passed or failed the tests and suggestions for improvement.

7. Software companies can invite participation from various user groups / stakeholders through *UniFace* while designing the GUI.
8. Testing through *UniFace* can be extremely helpful in ensuring that the GUI becomes a true cognitive mediator [18]. Cognitive stress on users and learning time can definitely be reduced to a certain extent.

ACKNOWLEDGEMENTS
I am grateful to Dr. Aaron Marcus, President, AM & A, USA for his encouraging feedback and supportiveness. I am thankful to Prof. Jan Gulliksen, Director of Studies (Human Computer Interaction), Dept. of Information Technology, Uppsala University, Sweden for his valuable suggestions. I acknowledge the valuable guidance of Dr. Mukul K. Sinha, my Ph.D. Supervisor and Managing Director of Expert Software Consultants, Pvt. Ltd. and the support of my group members at C-DAC.

REFERENCES
1. Baddeley, A. 'Your Memory' A Users Guide, Published by PRION, UK, (1996), 78-79.
2. Beaudouin-Lafon, M. User interface support for the integration of software tools: an iconic model of interaction, in Proceedings of the third ACM SIGSOFT/SIGPLAN software engineering symposium on Practical software development environments, (Boston, Massachusetts, United States, 1989), 143- 152.
3. Baecker, R., Small, I., and Mander R. Bringing icons to life, Proceedings of the SIGCHI conference on Human factors in computing systems: Reaching through technology (New Orleans, Louisiana, United States, March 1991), 1-6.
4. Byrne, D. M. Using Icons to Find Documents: Simplicity Is Critical, In the Proceedings of INTERCHI, (Amsterdam, The Netherlands, April 1993), 446-453.
5. Brami, R. Icons: A Unique Form of Painting, ACM Interactions, (Sept. + Oct. 1997), 15-28.
6. Britton, Jr. D., and Reyes, A. Discovering Usability Improvements for Mosaic: Application of the Contextual Inquiry Technique with an Expert User, The Second International WWW Conference '94: Mosaic and the Web Electronic Proceedings, 1994. Available at http://archive.ncsa.uiuc.edu/SDG/IT94/Proceedings/HCI/britton/britton_reyes.html
7. Carroll, M. J. Introduction: Human Computer Interaction, the Past and the Present, Human Computer Interaction in the New Millennium,

Published by ACM Press and Addison-Wesley, 2002.

8. *Fischer, G.* Beyond Couch Potatoes: From Consumers to Designers, Third Asian Pacific Computer & Human Interaction Conference Proceedings, (Kanagawa, Japan, July 1998), 15-17.

9. Giordano, R. and Bell, D. Participant Stakeholder Evaluation as a Design Process, in Conference Proceedings of ACM Universal Usability, (2000), 53-60.

10. Hemenway, K. Psychological issues in the use of icons in command menus, In the Conference Proceedings of the SIGCHI conference on Human factors in computing systems, (Gaithersburg, Maryland, United States, 1982), 20-23.

11. Holtzblatt, K., and Beyer, H. Apprenticing with the Customer: A collaborative Approach to Requirements Definition, in Electronic Proceedings of Communications of the ACM, (May 1995).

12. Holloway, J., and Bailey, J. Don't Use a Product's Developers for Icon Testing, in Proceedings of CHI '96, (Vancouver, British Columbia, Canada, April 1996), 309-310.

13. Howthorn, D. Possible Implications of Aging for Interface Designers, Interacting with Computers 12, Elsevier Science, (2000), 507-528.

14. Ivory, M., and Hearst, M. The state of the art in automating usability evaluation of user interfaces, ACM Computing Surveys (CSUR), Volume 33, Issue 4 (December 2001), 470-516.

15. Katherine, H. Why icons cannot stand alone, ACM SIGDOC Asterisk Journal of Computer Documentation, Volume 20, Issue 2 (May 1996), 1-8.

16. Katre, D., Unconventional Inspirations for Creating Software Interface Metaphors, in Proceedings of International Conference on Media and Design (Mumbai, India, Sept. 2002), Volume I, 1-15.

17. Lackoff, G., Metaphors We Live By, Published by Cambridge Press, (1990).

18. Laurel, B. Computers as Theatre, Published by Addison-Wesley, 1993, 7th Edition in 1999.

19. Marcus, A., Icons, symbols, and signs: visible languages to facilitate communication, ACM Interactions, Volume 10 , Issue 3 (May + June 2003), 37 - 43

20. Marcus, A., Armitage, J., and Frank, V. Globalization of User-Interface Design for the Web, 5th Conference on Human Factors and the Web, in Electronic Proceedings, (1999) Available at http://zing.ncsl.nist.gov/hfweb/proceedings/marcus/index.html

21. Miller, G.A., The magical number seven, plus or minus two: Some limits on our capacity for processing information, The Psychological Review, (1956), 81-97.

22. Molich, R., Bevan, N., Curson, I., Butler, S., Kindlund, E., Miller, D., and Kirakowski, J. Comparative evaluation of usability tests, in Proceedings of the Conference on Human Factors and Computing Systems, (CHI 1999), 83 – 84.

23. Nielsen, J. Why GUI panic is good panic, Interactions, Volume 1, Issue 2 (April 1994), 55 - 58.

24. Nielsen, J., Offshore Usability, Alertbox, Useit.com, Septmember 16, 2002, Available at http://www.useit.com/alertbox/20020916.html

25. Poovaiah, R., Graphics Symbols for Environmental Signage: A Design Perspective, in A design Perspective, IDC Publication, March 1997, IIT Bombay, 29-42.

26. Potosnak, K. (Editor), Do icons make user interfaces easier to use?, Human Factors, (May 1988), 97-99.

27. Redish, J., Bias, R., Bailey, R., Molich, R., Dumas, J., and Spool, J. , Conference on Human Factors and Computing Systems, (2002), 885 - 890.

28. Rowley, E., Usability testing in the field: bringing the laboratory to the user, Conference proceedings on Human factors in computing systems, 1994, 252 – 257.

29. Schaffer, E., and Sorflaten, J. ICONS: Much Ado About Something, Human Factors International, UI Design Update e-Newsletter, (December 1998), Available at http://www.humanfactors.com/library/icons.asp

30. Shneiderman, B., and Mahajan, R. Visual and Textual Consistency Checking Tools for Graphical User Interfaces, IEEE Transactions of Software Engineering, Vol. 23, No. 11, (November 1997), 722-735.

31. Sutcliffe, A. On the effective use and reuse of HCI knowledge, ACM Transactions on Computer-Human Interaction (TOCHI), Volume 7, Issue 2 (June 2000), 197 – 221.

32. Wolff, J. A Study of the Effect of Context Aand Test Method in Evaluating Safety Symbols, Georgia Institute of Technology, Graphics Visualization and Usability Centre's Report No. GIT-GVU-96-07, 1996.

K.   Viability of the Process

The proposed process for visualization of interface metaphor is used as part of following two live projects. It required approximately 15 to 16% and 8 to 9% of resources respectively depending upon the size of project and rendering style of interface metaphors.

Table K1. Resource Allocation (A)			
Project: 3D Game for Watershed		**Total Effort:** 120 Man months	
Common Knowledge Dimension: Day-to-day and Professional		**Class of metaphors used:** Diverse	
Rendering Style: Realistic			
Activities	**Roles**	**No. Persons**	**Man-months**
Interface Play Script (IPS)	Interface Designers	2	1.5
Identification, Classification, Categorization, Assessment, Selection	Interface Designer	1	2.0
Tuning Analysis of Candidate Interface Metaphors	Interface Designer	1	2.0
Quantitative Evaluation	Interface Designer	1	
Heuristic Evaluation	Interface Designer	1	1.0
Multimedia Rendering	Interface Designers	2	8.0
Usability Tests	Usability Expert Interface Designer	2	1.0
Modifications as per Test Results	Interface Designers	2	2.0
Acceptance Usability Tests	Usability Expert	1	1.0
Creation of UDL and ADL	Interface Designers	2	Continuous
Total Effort for Visualization of Interface Metaphor			**18.5 Man-months**
Approx. 15 to 16 % resources are utilized for implementing the visualization process of interface metaphor.			

Table K1. Resource Allocation (B)			
Project: JATAN Virtual Museum Builder		**Total Effort:** 30 Man months	
Common Knowledge Dimension: Professional		**Class of metaphors used:** Coherent	
Rendering Style: Optimized rendering with greater emphasis on integration at conceptual level			
Activities	**Roles**	**No. Persons**	**Man months**
Interface Play Script (IPS)	Interface Designer	1	15 Man days
Identification, Classification, Categorization, Assessment, Selection	Interface Designer	1	15 Man days
Tuning Analysis of Candidate Interface Metaphors	Interface Designer	1	15 Man days
Quantitative Evaluation	Interface Designer	1	10 Man days
Heuristic Evaluation	Interface Designer	1	2 Man days
Multimedia Rendering	Interface Designer	1	10 Man days
Usability Tests	Usability Expert Interface Designer	2	3 Man days
Modifications as per Test Results	Interface Designer	1	5 Man days
Acceptance Usability Test	Usability Expert	1	3 Man days
Creation of UDL and ADL	Interface Designer	1	Continuous
Total Effort for Visualization of Interface Metaphor			**2.6 Man-months**
Approx. 8 to 9 % resources are utilized for implementing the visualization process of interface metaphor.			

L. Background Information

The author of this dissertation has carried out all the experiments and case studies as part of live projects. This was necessary for ensuring the practicability of the process. The background information of these projects is provided in this section for the readers.

L1. Inscript Typing Tutor

Inscript Typing Tutor is designed for school children and professionals. It introduces the InScript Keyboard (specially designed for typing of Indian scripts) and use of appropriate fingers for typing the characters. It provides a separate module for introducing the basic letterforms (through animations indicating how to draw the letterforms). It includes interactive games for improving the typing skills of learners. Lessons for learning to type using Indian scripts and testing mechanisms for evaluating the performance are supported [Katre, 2005]

L2. JATAN: Virtual Museum Builder

It is a digital library solution for museums named JATAN: Virtual Museum Builder. It includes Integration, Management, Presentation, Administration and Subscription modules to help the data entry operators and curators in processing the records pertaining to museum collections. JATAN is designed to address specific requirements pertaining to digitization, data entry, data verification, approval, rights management, web publishing, access control etc. It can integrate museum artifacts as well as manuscripts.

L3. Multimedia Rendering of Dnyaneshwari

Dnyaneshwari is considered as one of the most profound commentaries on *Bhagvadgita* (A *Hindu* religious book). Saint *Dnyaneshwar* wrote it around 700 years ago. Multimedia rendering of Dnyaneshwari is produced in the form of two CD Titles. The CDs include translation and musical recitation with accurate pronunciations of Marathi and Sanskrit verses by *Sri Sakhare Maharaj*. The text is displayed in specially designed fonts. The user is able to read the text and listen to the recitation of verses for every page of Dnyaneshwari. Using multimedia over 40 metaphoric verses are visualized and rendered from the first chapter of *Dnyaneshwari*. All the contents are presented with a very attractive User Interface.

L4. QuickMM Album Authoring Tool

QuickMM Album Authoring Tool provides a pre-authored template, designed to suit specific topics and applications presented in multimedia. The basic authoring template structure is used for integrating multimedia contents and incorporates predefined locations and fields for integrating images, text, audio and video clips. QuickMM Album Authoring software enables semi-skilled professionals multimedia applications. Presently, it focuses on production of multimedia albums.

L5. Kumar Vishwa Kosha CD Title

It is basically a multimedia encyclopedia in Marathi (Local Language of Maharashtra State) designed for students in the age group of 10 -16 years.

L6. 3D Game for Watershed

3D Game is being developed for teaching watershed management techniques to villagers. In this game, we propose to simulate 3D terrain walkthrough of the village selected for watershed. The volunteers from this village play the proposed game. They can learn and apply the watershed treatments on the simulation of the terrain and see the results. This project is referred as '3D Game for Watershed' in the thesis.

M. Glossary of New Terminologies

The newly conceived terminologies in this dissertation are enlisted along with their definitions in this section.

Chapter 2.

1. Reference domain

Reference domain is the other entity with which the software is being compared.

2. Application domain

Application domain is the software for which the user interface is being designed.

Chapter 3.

3. Unmanifested Metaphor State

In the beginning of software project, many times, user interface designer is clueless about which metaphor will be suitable. The list of software requirements is not indicative enough. (S)he is stuck up thinking about how to identify the metaphor. This state of metaphor is called as 'unmanifested metaphor state'.

4. Manifested Metaphor State

In some cases, the candidate metaphor immediately clicks to the user interface designer. At times, (s)he foresees the probable metaphor even before starting to elicit software requirements. In some occasions, the customer explicitly suggests the desired interface metaphor. This state is called as 'manifested metaphor state'.

5. Commentary of Task Performance (CTP)

It is a narrative documentation of tasks performed by the users. It includes details of situations, options, goals, actions, decisions, activity and the outcome. It mentions all non-trivial and trivial objects used for completing the task and the purpose for which they were used. The sensory cues in terms of visual, verbal and auditory indications referred for predicting the status of the task are documented as part of CTP.

6. Interface Play Script (IPS)

It is to visualize and document how the user would perform the conventional task using the proposed software.

7. Coherent Interface Metaphors

Interface metaphors having some interrelation or any other common aspect are called coherent interface metaphors.

8. Diverse Interface Metaphors

Interface metaphors not having any interrelation or commonality are called diverse interface metaphors.

9. Inanimate Metaphor

This type of candidate interface metaphor represents the inanimate entity (objects) from the users' work environment. Such inanimate entities are called as inanimate metaphors.

10. Animate Metaphor

This type of candidate interface metaphor represents the animate entity (humans) from the users' work environment. Such animate entities are called as animate metaphors.

11. Domain Conceptual Structure

A domain is basically a large sphere of activities, which provides a very complex and rich conceptual structure.

12. Conglomerate Conceptual Structure

It is a conceptual structure of such interface metaphor that integrates several environments or groups of conceptual structures together.

13. Multitudinous Conceptual Structure

The user interface designer can select an environment that includes multiple entities (animate and inanimate), e.g., Desktop, Library, Gallery, Office Cabin, Classroom, Doctor's Clinic, Studio, etc. Such metaphoric environments provide multitudinous conceptual structures.

14. Singleton Conceptual Structure

Both animate and inanimate metaphors have singleton conceptual structures. It is a single hierarchy of concepts.

15. Flat Concept

The concept at the terminus of a branch within the conceptual structure is called as flat concept.

Chapter 4.

16. Tuning of Interface Metaphor

Adjusting the aspects of interface metaphor to satisfy the usability objectives and usability requirements of the software.

17. Conceptual Resonance

Re-echoing of concepts due to similarity between the source and the target in a metaphoric application.

Chapter 5.

18. Unmapped Concepts (UCs)

Concepts not corresponding with the listed software requirements are called unmapped concepts.

19. Unmapped Requirements (URs)

Software requirements not mapping with the interface metaphor are called unmapped requirements.

20. Dissection Termination (DT) point

The point where the user interface designer stops dissecting the interface metaphor.

21.Terminus Concept

Endpoint of a branch within the conceptual structure is called as the terminus concept.

22.Core Metaphor

The metaphor that focuses on main objectives of software while using diverse metaphors is called as core metaphor.

23.Supporting Metaphors

Usually, in case of diverse metaphors, the core metaphor is inadequate to represent all software requirements. In order to map the URs, user interface designer takes help of other metaphors. These are called as supporting metaphors.

24.Cooperative Integration

If the diverse interface metaphors are designed with a core interface metaphor at the center and supporting interface metaphors around it then this can be called as a cooperative integration.

25.Incoherent Integration

If the diverse interface metaphors are integrated without any logical connection or the design of core and supporting interface metaphors then it can be called as incoherent integration.

26.Conceptual Proximity

Conceptual proximity means, conceptual closeness between the core and supporting metaphors.

27.Conceptual Alignment

Highlighting certain aspects of the supporting metaphor while representing the unmapped requirements and maintaining conceptual relation with the core metaphor.

Chapter 6.

28. Conceptual Bandwidth

The total number of concepts emerged out of the dissection of interface metaphor are called as its conceptual bandwidth.

29. Usable Conceptual Bandwidth

The total number of Cross-Domain Mappings (CDMs) formed during the dissection activity defines the usable conceptual bandwidth of interface metaphor.

30. Coverage of Interface Metaphor

This is the percentage of software requirements mapped with the interface metaphor.

Chapter 7.

31. User Domain Lexicon (UDL)

The collection of vocabulary associated with the interface metaphor and the tasks performed by the users.

32. Application Domain Lexicon (ADL)

The collection of vocabulary used as part of user interface by the software developer.

Chapter 8.

33. Conceptual Cluster

Abstract ideas held together as a group.

Chapter 9.

34. Usability Indicator

The qualitative, observable signs or specific pointers of usability.

Chapter 10.

35. Diffusion of Interface Metaphor

The diffusion of interface metaphor describes the gradation of rendering and depiction of interface metaphor in the software in terms of moderate, optimized, conceptual, behavioral / functional.

References

A

Apple (2004). Introduction to the Apple Human Interface Guidelines
Retrieved on July 5th, 2004 from
http://developer.apple.com/documentation/UserExperience/Conceptual/OSXHIGuidelines/index.html

B

Back M, Cohen J, Gold R, Harrison S, Minneman S (2001). Listen reader: an electronically augmented paper-based book, Proceedings of the SIGCHI conference on Human factors in computing systems, pp. 23–29.

Barnard P (2000). The contributions of Applied Cognitive Psychology To The Study of HCI, Readings in HCI: Towards the year 2000, Edited by Baecker R, Grudin J, Buxton W, Greenberg S, Published by Morgan Kaufmann, II Edition, pp. 640-658.

Barr P, Biddle R, Noble J (2002). A Taxonomy of User-Interface Metaphors, In Proceedings of SIGCHI-NZ Symposium On Computer-Human Interaction (CHINZ 2002), Hamilton, New Zealand.

Berne E (1961). *Transactional Analysis in Psychotherapy*. Grove Press, Inc., New York, 1961. Page 13.

Beyer H, Haltzblatt K (1996). Contextual Techniques, Interactions (6)1, pp. 32-42.

Bias R (1991). Walkthroughs: Efficient collaborative testing. IEEE Software, 8(5), 94-95.

Bizzozero S and Rana A (1994). Dynamic WAIS Book: an electronic book to publish and consult information distributed across a wide-area network, ACM AVI 1994, pp. 225-228.

Boehm B (1988). A spiral model of software development and enhancement, IEEE Computer 21(2), pp. 61-72.

Boring R (2002). HUMAN-COMPUTER INTERACTION AS COGNITIVE SCIENCE, PROCEEDINGS of the HUMAN FACTORS AND ERGONOMICS SOCIETY 46th ANNUAL MEETING, pp. 1768-1771.

Brad B (1990). Strategies for Automatically Incorporating Metaphoric Attributes in Interface Designs. Proceedings of the third annual ACM SIGGRAPH symposium on User Interface Software and Technology. ACM Press, New York, USA, pp. 66-75.

C

Card S, Hong L, Mackinlay J, Chi E (2004a). 3Book: A Scalable 3D Virtual Book, In the proceedings of CHI 2004, pp. 1095-1098.

Card S, Hong L, Mackinlay J, Chi E (2004b). 3Book: A 3D electronic smart book, In Proceedings of AVI 2004, pp. 303-307.

Carroll J, Mack R, and Kellogg W (1988). Interface metaphors and user interface design, In Handbook of Human-Computer Interaction, Helander, M. (Editor), Elsevier Science Publishers B.V.: North-Holland, pp. 67- 85.

Carroll J (2002). Introduction: Human Computer Interaction, the Past and the Present, Human Computer Interaction in the New Millennium, Published by ACM Press and Addison-Wesley, USA.

Chandler D (1994). Semiotics for Beginners
Retrieved on 13th Oct. 2004 from
http://www.aber.ac.uk/media/Documents/S4B/semiotic.html

Chandler D (1997). Visual Perception
Retrieved on 13th Oct. 2004 from
http://www.aber.ac.uk/media/Modules/MC10220/visindex.html

Chater N, Vitanyi P (2003). Simplicity: A unifying principle in cognitive science? Trends in Cognitive Sciences Volume 7, Number 1, pp. 19-22.

Chen D, Wong A, Jackie J (2002). Dimensions of Metaphor Consistency in Computer-Based Learning (CBL) Design: Lessons Learned from Project Justice Bao, Journal of Educational Multimedia and Hypermedia, 11(3), pp. 251-266.

Chu Y, Bainbridge D, Jones M, Witten I (2004). Realistic books: a bizarre homage to an obsolete medium?, Proceedings of the 2004 joint ACM/IEEE conference on Digital libraries, pp. 78–86.

Clair R. N., Visual metaphor, Cultural Knowledge and the Rhetoric, Learn In Beauty: Indigenous Education for a New Century, Published by Northern Arizona University, (2000), pp. 85-101.

Cognitive Ergonomics and Engineering Psychology, Ergonomics Today, June 11, 2001.
Retrieved on Jan. 31, 2005 from
http://www.ergoweb.com/news/detail.cfm?id=352

Cooper A (1994). The Perils of Prototyping, Visual Basic Programmer's Journal, Aug/Sept 1994.
Retrieved on 13 Oct. 2004 from
http://www.cooper.com/articles/art_perils_of_prototyping.htm

D

Dieberger A, Frank A (1998), A city metaphor for supporting navigation in complex information spaces, Journal of Visual Languages and Computing, 1998 (9), pp. 597-622.
Retrieved on 21 March 2005 from
http://homepage.mac.com/juggle5/WORK/publications/JVisLang_City.html

Dix A, Finlay J, Gregory D, Abowd, beale R (2004). Human Computer Interaction, Published by Pearson Education, USA.

Duncker E (2002). Cross Cultural Usability of Library Metaphor, In Proceedings of JCDL 2002, pp. 223-230.

E

Erickson, T. D., Interfaces and Evolution of Pidgins: Creative Design for the Analytically Inclined, The Art of Human-Computer Interface Design, Edited by Brenda Laurel in 1990, Published by Addison Wesley, USA, pp. 11.

Erickson, T (2000). Working with Interface Metaphors, Readings in HCI: Towards the year 2000, Edited by Baecker R, Grudin J, Buxton W, Greenberg S, Published by Morgan Kaufmann, II Edition, pp. 147-151.

Edvinsson L, Malone S (1997). *Intellectual Capital: Realizing Your Company's True Value by Finding Its Hidden Brainpower*. New York: Harper Business, 1997, pp. 10-15.

G

Gasset J (1925). The Dehumanization of Art; and Other Essays on Art, Culture, and Literature, Trans. A. McVitty, Jr. Princeton University Press, 1968.

Gaver W (1995). Oh what a tangled web we weave: metaphor and mapping in graphical interfaces. CHI 95 Conference Companion 1995, pp. 270-271.

Götze M, Schlechtweg S (2003). Magic Pages - Providing Added Value to Electronic Documents". In: Constantine Stephanidis, Julie Jacko (eds.): Proceedings of HCI International 2003 (Crete, Greece, June 22-27, 2003), volume 2, pp. 651-655.

Gulliksen J (2001). The technical report of Usability Throughout SDLC: A Summary of Interact 2001 Workshop.

H

Hall P, Hudson R (1997). Software without Frontiers, a Multi-Platform, Multi-Cultural, Multi-Nation Approach. Wiley and Sons Chichester.

Hamilton A. (2000). Metaphor in Theory and Practice: the Influence of Metaphors on Expectations, ACM Journal of Computer Documentation November 2000/Vol. 24, No. 4, pp 237-253.

Hedberg J, Harper B (1992). Creating interface metaphors for interactive multimedia, Electronic *Proceedings of the International Interactive Multimedia Symposium (IIMS)*, Perth, Western Australia, Published by Promaco Conventions Pvt. Ltd.
Retrieved on 31 Jan. 2005 from
http://www.aset.org.au/confs/iims/1992/iims92-conts.html

Henke H (1998). Are Electrons Better Than Papyrus? (Or Can Adobe Acrobat Reader Files Replace Hardcopy?), pp. 29-37.

Holtzblatt K, Beyer H (1995). Apprenticing with the Customer: A collaborative Approach to Requirements Definition, in Electronic Proceedings of Communications of the ACM.

Hudson W (2000). Metaphor: A Double-Edged Sword, ACM Interactions, May + June 2000, pp. 11-15.

I

ISO/IEC FDIS 9126-1: Software Engineering - Product quality - Part 1: Quality model (2000).

J

Jha V (1998). The Grammar of Metaphor: An Indian Approach, In the Proceedings of the National Seminar on Metaphors in Vedic Literature, Published by Center for Advanced Study in Sanskrit, University of Pune, India, pp. 137-140.

Johnson-Laird N (1980). Mental Models in Cognitive Science, Cognitive Science 4, pp. 71-115.

Johnson J, Roberts T, Verplank W, Smith D, Irby C, Beard M, Nackey K (Originally published in 1989). Republished in Readings in Human-Computer Interaction: Toward the Year 2000, Baecker R, Grudin J, Buxton W, Greenberg S (2000) by Morgan Kaufmann Publishers, USA, pp. 53-70.

Judge A (1991). Metaphors as Transdisciplinary Vehicles of the Future, In Proceedings of Conference on Science and Tradition: Transdisciplinary Perspectives on the way to the 21st Century organized with UNESCO.
Retrieved in July 2004 from
http://www.laetusinpraesens.org/docs/transveh.php

K

Kahn M and Prail A (1994). Formal usability inspections. In Nielsen & Mack (Eds.), Usability Inspection Methods. New York: John Wiley & Sons, 141-171.

Kass R, Finin T (1988). A General User Modeling Facility. Conference proceedings on Human Factors in Computing Systems, 145-150.

Katre D (1999). Multimedia Rendering of Spiritual Texts, Proceedings of International Conference Virtual Systems and Multimedia (VSMM 1999), University of Abertay, Dandee, Scotland, UK., pp. 500-507.

Katre D (2001). Template based Authoring for Cost Effective Multimedia Production, IEEE Multimedia Technology and Applications International Conference Proceedings, University of California, Irvine, USA, Nov. 2001, pp. 133-142.

Katre D (2002). Unconventional Inspirations for Creating Software Interface Metaphors, in Proceedings of International Conference on Media and Design (Mumbai, India, Sept. 2002), Volume I, 1-15.

Katre D (2003). My Interface Representation of Requisite System (MIRORS), From Mono-GUI to Multi-GUI, A prize winning article submitted for the GUI of the Future Contest' of PC Quest in August 2003.

Katre D (2004a). Pragmatic and Usable Approach for Digital Library Initiatives in India, Proceedings of International Conference on Digital Libraries (ICDL), New Delhi, India, Volume I, pp. 41-48.

Katre D, Puntamkar S, Gajbhiye J (2004b). Design and Development of JATAN: Virtual Museum Builder, In Proceedings of NACLIN 2004, India, pp. 247-257.

Katre D (2004c). Using Mnemonic Techniques as part of Pictorial Interface for Self Identification of Illiterate Villagers, In Proceedings of International Conference on Human Computer Interaction (I-HCI 2004) organized by IESUP and CSI, Bangalore, India.

Katre D (2005). Juxtaposing Commentary of Task Performance (CTP) and Interface Play Script (IPS) for Discovering Interface Metaphors, In Proceedings of International Conference on Information Management (ICIM), Mumbai, India, Volume II, pp. 809-818.

Katre D (2005). Designing the Teacher Like Behavior of e-Learning System: A Case Study of Indian Scripts Typing Tutor, I-Manager's International Journal of Education Technology, Oct-Dec. 2005, Volume 2, No.3, pp. 60-65.

Kearney A, Kaplan S (1997). Toward A Methodology For The Measurement Of Knowledge Structures Of Ordinary People: The Conceptual Content Cognitive Map (3CM), Environment and Behaviour, Vol. 29, Issue 5, pp579, ISSN: 0013-9165.

KeeBook Creator 2.7 Education Demo Version
Retrieved on July 5th, 2004 from http://www.keebook.com

L

Lakoff G and Johnson M (1980). Metaphors We Live By, Cambridge Press, USA.

Landy J and Mayers B (1995). Just Draw it! Programming by Sketching Storyboards, HCI Technical Report, School of Computer Science, Carnegie Mellon University , USA, (Nov. 1995).

Lewis C and Rieman J (1994). Task-Centered User Interface Design: A Practical Introduction
Retrieved on 13 Oct. 2004 from
http://hcibib.org/tcuid/

Lundell (1995). Designing a "Front Panel" for Unix: The Evolution of a Metaphor, In the electronic proceedings of CHI 1995, ACM Press.

Laurel, B. (1993). Computers as Theatre, Addison-Wesley, USA.

M

McInerney P and Sobiesiak R (2000). The UI Design Process, Planning, Managing, and Documenting UI Design Work, SIGCHI Bulletin, Volume 32, Number 1, (January 2000), pp. 17-21.

Madsen K (1994). A Guide to Metaphor Design, Communications of the ACM, December 1994/ Vol. 37/ No. 12., ACM Press, New York, USA. pp. 57-62.

Madsen K (2000). Magic by Metaphors, In proceedings of DARE 2000, pp 167-170.

Mander M, Salomon G, Wong Y (1992). A "pile" metaphor for supporting casual organization of information, Proceedings of the SIGCHI conference on Human factors in computing systems table of contents, pp. 627–634.

Marchak M (2000). The Magic of Visual Interaction Design, The SIGCHI Bulletin, ACM Press, Volume 32, Number 2, April 2000.

Marcus A (1993). Human Communications Issues in UIs, Communications of The ACM, April 1993 / Vol. 36, No. 4, pp. 101-109.

Marcus A (1994). Managing Metaphors for Advanced User Interfaces, In the Proceedings of the workshop on Advanced Visual Interfaces 1994, ACM Press, New York, USA, pp. 12-18.

Marcus A (1995). Metaphor Design in User Interfaces: How to Effectively Manage Expectation, Surprise, Comprehension, and Delight, In the Proceedings of CHI'95 MOSAIC OF CREATIVITY, 1995, pp. 373-374.

Marcus A (1998). Metaphor Design in User Interfaces, Journal of Computer Documentation, Vol.22, No.2, pp. 43-57.

Marcus A (2002). Metaphors and User Interfaces in the 21st Century, Interactions of ACM, Volume IX.2, pp. 7-10.

Marcus A (2002). Dare We Define User-Interface Design?, Interactions of ACM, September - October, 2002, pp. 19-24.

Marshall C, Price M, Golovchinsky G, Schilit B (2001). Designing e-Books for Legal Research, In proceedings of JCDL, 2001, pp. 41-48.

Microsoft (2004). The User Interface Guidelines for Microsoft Windows
Retrieved on July 5th, 2004 from
http://msdn.microsoft.com/library/default.asp?url=/library/enus/vccore98/html/_cor
e_the_user_interface_guidelines_for_microsoft_windows.asp

Mohnkern K (1997). Visual Interaction Design: Beyond the Interface Metaphor, SIGCHI Bulletin, Vol.29 No.2, April 1997.

Moll-Carrillo H, Salomon G, Marsh M, Suri J, Spreenberg P (1995). Articulating a Metaphor Through User-Centered Design, In the electronic proceedings of CHI 1995, ACM Press.

Moser K (2000). Metaphor Analysis in psychology-Method, theory, and Fields of Application, Forum Qualitative Social Research On-line Journal, Volume 1, No. 2.

Mountford S (2000). Tools and Techniques for Creative Design, Readings in HCI: Towards the year 2000, Edited by Baecker R, Grudin J, Buxton W, Greenberg S, Published by Morgan Kaufmann, II Edition, pp. 129-141.

N

Nielsen J, Molich R (1990). Heuristic evaluation of user interfaces, *Proc. ACM CHI'90 Conf.* (Seattle, WA, 1-5 April), 249-256.

Nielsen J (1994). Why GUI panic is good panic, Interactions, Volume 1, Issue 2 (April 1994), pp. 55-58.

Nielsen J (1998). Electronic books - a bad idea. Jakob Nielsen's Alertbox. 26 July 1998.

Norman D (1988). The Psychology of Everyday Things. Basic Books, New York, USA, 1988. (In paperback as The Design of Everyday Things. Doubleday, New York, USA1990).

Norman D (1999). Conventions, and Design, ACM Interactions, May+ June 1999, pp. 38-41.

O

Owen G, (1999) SIGGRAPH, Definitions and Rationale for Visualization
Retrieved on 10th Oct. 2004 from
www.siggraph.org/education/ materials/HyperVis/visgoals/visgoal2.htm

P

Palmquist, Ruth A (1996). The Search for an Internet Metaphor: A Comparison of Literatures. ASIS Conference Proceedings.

Press L (2000). From P-books to E-books, Communications of the ACM, May 2000/Vol.43, No. 5, pp.17-21.

Pressman R (2001). Software Engineering A Practitioner's Approach", Fifth International Edition, McGRAW-HILL, New York, USA.

Polson P, Lewis C, Rieman J, Wharton C (1992). Cognitive Walkthroughs: A method for theory based evaluation of user interfaces, International Journal of Man-Machine Studies, 36:741-73.

Poovaiah R (1994). Seminar on 'Design Odyssey', November 1994, Industrial Design Center, Indian Institute of Technology, Bombay, India.

R

Redish J, Bias R, Bailey R, Molich R, Dumas J, and Spool J (2002). Conference on Human Factors and Computing Systems, 885 - 890.

Richards, I.A. 1936. *The Philosophy of Rhetoric*. Oxford: Clarendon Press.

Richard M (1941). The Basic Works of Aristotle, Trans, New York: Random House Inc., 1941.

Rieman J, Franzke M and Redmiles D (1995). Usability Evaluation with the Cognitive Walkthrough, In the Proceedings of CHI'95.

Roget's Thesaurus (1990). Published by Doubleday and Company Inc. NY, USA.

Rudd J, Stern K and Isensee S (1996). Low vs. high fidelity prototyping debate. Interactions 3(1),ACM Press, pp. 76-85.

Russell J (2001). Book Metaphor: Friend or Foe?, ACM SIGDOC 2001, 180-185.

S

Sears, A. (1997). Heuristic Walkthroughs: Finding the Problems Without the Noise. International Journal of Human-Computer Interaction, 9(3), 213-234.

Schneider G, Winters J (1999). Applying Use Cases: A Practical Guide, Published by Addison-Wesley, USA.

Shiratuddin N, Landoni M, Gibb F, Hassan S (2003). e-book Technology and Its Potential in Distance Education, Journal of Digital Information, Volume 3, Issue 4, Article 160
Retrieved on July 5th, 2004 from
http://jodi.ecs.soton.ac.uk/Articles/v03/i04/Shiratuddin/#sec62

Smilowitz E (1996). Do Metaphors Make Web Browsers Easier to Use?, Conference on Designing for the Web: Empirical Studies, Electronic Proceedings.

Sumner T, Bonnardel N, Kallak B (1997). The Cognitive Ergonomics of Knowledge-Based Design Support Systems, Proceedings of CHI'97, ACM Press, USA.

T

Toms E G and Campbell D G (1999). Genre as Interface Metaphor: Exploiting Form and Function in Digital Environments, Proceedings of the 32nd Hawaii International Conference on System Sciences - 1999, pp. 1-17.

Torenvliet G (2003). The whiteboard: We can't afford it! the devaluation of a usability term, ACM interactions Volume 10, Number 4, 2003, pp. 12-17.

V

Vaantinen K and Schmidt J (1994). User Interfaces for Hypermedia: How to Find Good Metaphors?, In the proceedings of Conference Companion CHI'94, ACM Press, pp. 263-264.

Vishwanāthanyāyapanchānan (17th Century A.D.). *Nyāyasiddhānt Muktāvali.*

W

Wade N and Swanston M (1991). Visual Perception: An Introduction, London: Routledge, pp. 212.

Weiner J. E. (1984). A Knowledge Representation Approach to Understanding Metaphors, Computational Linguistics, Volume 10, Number 1, January-March 1984, pp. 1-14.

Wharton C, Bradford J, Jeffries R and Franzke M (1992). Applying Cognitive Walkthroughs to More Complex User Interfaces: Experiences, Issues, and Recommendations. Proceedings of CHI Conference on Human Factors in Computing Systems. New York: ACM, 381-388.

Wilcox P (2001). Metaphors in American Sign Language, Published by Gallaudet University Press.

Wilson D, Rauch T and Paige J (1992). Prototyping in the Software Development Cycle" drawn from a number of sources at the ACM CHI '92 conference, May 1992 Retrieved on 13th Oct., 2004 from
http://www.firelily.com/opinions/cycle.html

Wilson R (2001). Evolution of Portable Electronic Books. Ariadne, issue 29 Retrieved on July 5th, 2004 from
http://www.ariadne.ac.uk/issue29/wilson/

Wilson R (2002). The "Look and Feel" of an Ebook: Considerations in Interface Design, ACM SAC, 2002, pp. 530-535.

Wood L, Skrebowski L (2004). The Future's Here; It's Just Unevenly Distributed, ACM Interactions, March-April 2004, pp. 76-79.

Y

Yousef M (2001). Assessment of Metaphor Efficacy in User Interfaces for the Elderly: A Tentative Model for Enhancing Accessibility, In the proceedings of WUAUC'01, pp. 120-124.